FAVORITE BRAND NAME

BEST-LOVED
RECIPES
— of All Time —

PUBLICATIONS INTERNATIONAL, LTD.

Contents

Party Fare & Thirst Quenchers

Create any of these dazzling appetizers and drinks for a sure-fire taste extravaganza. Impress party guests or surprise your family with a special pre-dinner treat. Discover dozens of ways to make any occasion a smashing success.

Buffalo Chicken Wings

24 chicken wings
 1 teaspoon salt
¼ teaspoon ground black pepper
 4 cups vegetable oil for frying
¼ cup butter or margarine
¼ cup hot pepper sauce
 1 teaspoon white wine vinegar
   Celery sticks
 1 bottle (8 ounces) blue cheese
   dressing

Cut tips off wings at first joint; discard tips. Cut remaining wings into two parts at the joint; sprinkle with salt and pepper. Heat oil in deep fryer or heavy saucepan to 375°F. Add half the wings; fry about 10 minutes or until golden brown and crisp, stirring occasionally. Remove with slotted spoon; drain on paper towels. Repeat with remaining wings.

Melt butter in small saucepan over medium heat; stir in pepper sauce and vinegar. Cook until thoroughly heated. Place wings on large platter. Pour sauce over wings. Serve warm with celery and dressing for dipping.
Makes 24 appetizers

*Favorite recipe from **National Broiler Council***

Buffalo Chicken Wings

Deluxe Fajita Nachos

2½ cups shredded, cooked chicken
1 package (1.27 ounces) LAWRY'S®
    Spices & Seasonings for Fajitas
⅓ cup water
8 ounces tortilla chips
1¼ cups (5 ounces) grated Cheddar
    cheese
1 cup (4 ounces) grated Monterey Jack
    cheese
1 large tomato, chopped
1 can (2¼ ounces) sliced ripe olives,
    drained
¼ cup sliced green onions
    Salsa
    Guacamole
    Dairy sour cream

In medium skillet, combine chicken, Spices & Seasonings and water; blend well. Bring to a boil; reduce heat and simmer 7 minutes. In large, shallow ovenproof platter, arrange chips. Top with chicken and cheeses. Place under broiler to melt cheese. Top with tomato, olives, green onions and desired amount of salsa. *Makes 4 appetizer servings or 2 main-dish servings*

Presentation: Garnish with guacamole, sour cream and salsa.

Substitution: Use 1¼ pounds cooked ground beef in place of shredded chicken.

Hint: For spicier nachos, add sliced jalapeños.

Chicken Saté

Chicken Kabobs (recipe follows)
1 teaspoon MAZOLA® Corn Oil
1 teaspoon dark Oriental sesame oil
¼ cup finely chopped onion
1 clove garlic, minced
½ teaspoon grated fresh ginger
¼ teaspoon crushed red pepper
    (optional)
½ cup SKIPPY® Creamy Peanut Butter
¼ cup KARO® Light or Dark Corn Syrup
1 tablespoon soy sauce
1 tablespoon cider vinegar
⅔ cup milk

Begin preparing Chicken Kabobs. Meanwhile, in small saucepan heat oils over medium heat; add onion, garlic, ginger and red pepper. Stirring constantly, cook 3 to 4 minutes or until onion is translucent. Stir in peanut butter, corn syrup, soy sauce and vinegar until smooth. Gradually stir in milk. Stirring constantly, bring to a boil. Remove from heat. Cool slightly. Serve as dipping sauce for Chicken Kabobs.
Makes about 3 dozen appetizers

Chicken Kabobs: Soak about 36 wooden skewers in water at least 20 minutes. In medium bowl combine 2 tablespoons Mazola® Corn Oil and 2 tablespoons light teriyaki sauce. Cut 1 pound boneless skinless chicken breasts into 1-inch pieces; stir into teriyaki mixture. Cover and let stand at room temperature no longer than 30 minutes or refrigerate several hours or overnight.

Thread chicken onto skewers. Place on foil-lined baking sheet. Broil about 6 inches from heat, 6 to 8 minutes or until lightly browned.

Deluxe Fajita Nachos

Early handling and production process of walnuts, which have become a major California crop.
Photo courtesy of Walnut Marketing Board

Indian-Spiced Walnuts

   2 egg whites, lightly beaten
   1 tablespoon ground cumin
1½ teaspoons salt
1½ teaspoons curry powder
   ½ teaspoon sugar
   4 cups walnut halves and pieces

Coat large, shallow baking pan with nonstick vegetable spray. Mix egg whites with seasonings. Stir in walnuts and coat thoroughly. Spread in prepared pan. Bake in 350°F oven 15 to 18 minutes, until dry and crisp. Cool completely before serving.

Makes 4 cups

*Favorite recipe from **Walnut Marketing Board***

Spicy Toasted Nuts

2 tablespoons vegetable oil
1 tablespoon HEINZ® Worcestershire
   Sauce
1 cup pecan or walnut halves

In bowl, combine oil and Worcestershire sauce; add nuts and toss to coat. Spread nuts in shallow baking pan; drizzle with any remaining oil mixture. Bake in 325°F oven, 15 minutes, stirring occasionally. Sprinkle with salt or garlic salt, if desired.

Makes 1 cup

Original Chex® Brand Party Mix

¼ cup margarine or butter, melted
4½ teaspoons Worcestershire sauce
1¼ teaspoons seasoned salt
 8 cups of your favorite CHEX® brand
   cereals (Corn, Rice and/or Wheat)
 1 cup mixed nuts
 1 cup pretzels

1. Preheat oven to 250°F.

2. Combine margarine, Worcestershire sauce and seasoned salt; mix well. Pour cereals, nuts and pretzels into large resealable plastic food storage bag.

3. Pour margarine mixture over cereal mixture inside plastic bag. Seal top of bag securely. Shake bag until all pieces are evenly coated.

4. Pour contents of bag into open roasting pan. Bake 1 hour, stirring every 15 minutes. Spread on absorbent paper towels to cool. Store in airtight container.

Makes 10 cups

Microwave Directions:

1. Follow steps 2 and 3 above.

2. Pour contents of bag into large microwave-safe bowl. Microwave on HIGH 5 to 6 minutes, stirring thoroughly every 2 minutes. While stirring, make sure to scrape side and bottom of bowl. Cool and store as directed above.

Ralston Foods, Inc.

Through the years, Chex® cereal has changed shape and name, added several flavors and survived major wars and a depression. Today, this delicious breakfast food is also an important ingredient in many snack, dessert and main-dish recipes. According to legend, the famous Chex Party Mix, which uses Wheat, Rice and Corn Chex, first showed up at a social gathering in St. Louis in 1955. This tasty snack remains a party favorite even now.

Layered Taco Dip

1 pound lean ground beef
1 (4-ounce) can chopped green chilies, undrained
2 teaspoons WYLER'S® or STEERO® Beef-Flavor Instant Bouillon
1 (15- or 16-ounce) can refried beans
1 (16-ounce) container BORDEN® or MEADOW GOLD® Sour Cream
1 (1.7-ounce) package taco seasoning mix
Guacamole (recipe follows)
Garnishes: Shredded Cheddar or Monterey Jack cheese, chopped fresh tomatoes, sliced green onions, sliced ripe olives
LAFAMOUS® Tortilla Chips

In large skillet, brown beef; pour off fat. Add chilies and bouillon; cook and stir until bouillon dissolves. Cool. Stir in refried beans. In small bowl, combine sour cream and taco seasoning; set aside. In 7- or 8-inch springform pan or on large plate, spread beef mixture. Top with sour cream mixture then guacamole. Cover; chill several hours. Just before serving, remove side of springform pan and garnish as desired. Serve with tortilla chips. Refrigerate leftovers.
Makes 12 to 15 servings

Guacamole: In small bowl, mash 3 ripe avocados, pitted and peeled. Add ¾ cup chopped fresh tomato, 2 tablespoons REALEMON® Lemon Juice from Concentrate or REALIME® Lime Juice from Concentrate, ½ teaspoon seasoned salt and ⅛ teaspoon garlic salt; mix well. Makes about 2 cups.

Layered Taco Dip

Spicy Dijon Dip

1 (8-ounce) package cream cheese, softened
¼ cup GREY POUPON® Dijon or COUNTRY DIJON® Mustard
¼ cup dairy sour cream
1 tablespoon finely chopped green onion
1 (4¼-ounce) can tiny shrimp, drained or ½ cup cooked shrimp, chopped
Sliced green onions, for garnish
Assorted cut-up vegetables

In small bowl, with electric mixer at medium speed, blend cream cheese, mustard, sour cream and chopped onion; stir in shrimp. Cover; chill at least 2 hours. Garnish with sliced onions; serve as a dip with vegetables.
Makes 1½ cups

The mustard business, founded by an Englishman named Grey, flourished in the same French community for two centuries.
Photo courtesy of Nabisco, Inc.

French Onion Dip

1 container (16 ounces) sour cream
½ cup HELLMANN'S® or BEST FOODS®
Real or Light Mayonnaise or Low
Fat Mayonnaise Dressing
1 package (1.9 ounces) KNORR® French
Onion Soup and Recipe Mix

In medium bowl combine sour cream, mayonnaise and soup mix. Cover; chill. Serve with fresh vegetables or potato chips. Garnish as desired.

Makes about 2½ cups

Spinach Dip

1 package (10 ounces) frozen chopped
spinach, thawed and drained
1½ cups sour cream
1 cup HELLMANN'S® or BEST FOODS®
Real or Light Mayonnaise or Low
Fat Mayonnaise Dressing
1 package (1.4 ounces) KNORR®
Vegetable Soup and Recipe Mix
1 can (8 ounces) water chestnuts,
drained and chopped (optional)
3 green onions, chopped

In medium bowl combine spinach, sour cream, mayonnaise, soup mix, water chestnuts and green onions. Cover; chill. Serve with fresh vegetables, crackers or chips. Garnish as desired.

Makes about 3 cups

Cucumber Dill Dip

1 package (8 ounces) light cream
cheese, softened
1 cup HELLMANN'S® or BEST FOODS®
Real or Light Mayonnaise or Low
Fat Mayonnaise Dressing
2 medium cucumbers, peeled, seeded
and chopped
2 tablespoons sliced green onions
1 tablespoon lemon juice
2 teaspoons snipped fresh dill *or*
½ teaspoon dried dill weed
½ teaspoon hot pepper sauce

In medium bowl beat cream cheese until smooth. Stir in mayonnaise, cucumbers, green onions, lemon juice, dill and hot pepper sauce. Cover; chill. Serve with fresh vegetables, crackers or chips. Garnish as desired.   *Makes about 2½ cups*

The Famous Lipton® California Dip

1 envelope LIPTON® Recipe Secrets®
Onion Soup Mix
1 container (16 ounces) sour cream

In small bowl, blend onion soup mix with sour cream; chill.   *Makes about 2 cups dip*

California Seafood Dip: Add 1 cup finely chopped cooked clams, crabmeat or shrimp, ¼ cup chili sauce and 1 tablespoon horseradish.

Left to right: French Onion Dip,
Cucumber Dill Dip and Spinach Dip

Velveeta® Salsa Dip

Velveeta® Salsa Dip

**1 pound VELVEETA® Pasteurized
   Process Cheese Spread, cubed
1 (8-ounce) jar salsa or picante sauce
2 tablespoons chopped cilantro
   (optional)**

• Stir process cheese spread and salsa in saucepan on low heat until process cheese spread is melted. Stir in cilantro.

• Serve hot with tortilla chips or vegetable dippers.   *Makes 3 cups*

Variations:

Prepare Velveeta® Salsa Dip as directed, adding 1 (16-ounce) can refried beans.

Prepare Velveeta® Salsa Dip as directed, adding ½ pound chorizo or hot bulk pork sausage, cooked, drained.

Touch Down Taco Dip

1 (8-ounce) package cream cheese, softened
½ cup dairy sour cream
½ cup ORTEGA® Mild, Medium or Hot Thick and Smooth Taco Sauce
1 teaspoon chili powder
¼ teaspoon ground red pepper
½ cup chopped cucumber
¼ cup sliced scallions
Shredded lettuce, chopped tomato, sliced black olives, for garnish
MR. PHIPPS® Pretzel Chips

With electric mixer at medium speed, beat cream cheese and sour cream until smooth. Stir in taco sauce, chili powder and red pepper. Fold in cucumber and scallions. Chill at least 1 hour. To serve, spoon dip into center of large round plate; top with lettuce, tomato and olives. Arrange pretzel chips around edge of dip. Serve with additional pretzel chips for dipping.   *Makes 2½ cups*

Lobster Butter Log

½ pound cooked lobster, finely chopped
6 tablespoons butter, softened
1 teaspoon minced onion
½ teaspoon seasoned salt
¼ teaspoon paprika
½ cup chopped parsley

Combine all ingredients except parsley in medium bowl. Roll mixture in plastic wrap; roll into log shape. Refrigerate about 4 hours or until firm. Roll log in parsley and serve with crackers or melba toast.   *Makes 1¾ cups*

Favorite recipe from **Florida Department of Agriculture and Consumer Services, Bureau of Seafood and Aquaculture**

Hot Artichoke Spread

1 cup MIRACLE WHIP® Salad Dressing or KRAFT® Real Mayonnaise
1 cup (4 ounces) KRAFT® 100% Grated Parmesan Cheese
1 (14-ounce) can artichoke hearts, drained, chopped

• Heat oven to 350°F.

• Mix all ingredients; spoon into 9-inch pie plate or 2-cup casserole.

• Bake 20 minutes or until lightly browned. Garnish as desired. Serve with tortilla chips, crackers or party rye bread slices.
Makes about 2 cups

Raspberry Mint Cooler

1 to 2 cups fresh mint leaves
5 cups DOLE® Pineapple Juice, chilled
2 cups DOLE® Fresh or Frozen Raspberries
1 can (6 ounces) frozen limeade concentrate, thawed
1 bottle (32 ounces) lemon-lime soda, chilled
1 lime, thinly sliced for garnish (optional)

• Rub mint leaves around side of punch bowl, then drop the bruised leaves in bottom of bowl.

• Combine remaining ingredients in punch bowl. *Makes 15 servings*

Kokomo Quencher

2 bottles (32 ounces each) lemon-lime soda, chilled
1 bottle (40 ounces) DOLE® Pure & Light Orchard Peach Juice, chilled
5 cups DOLE® Pineapple Juice, chilled
2 cups fresh or frozen blackberries
1 can (15 ounces) real cream of coconut
1 lime, thinly sliced for garnish

• Combine all ingredients in large punch bowl. *Makes 28 servings*

Sunlight Sipper

1½ cups DOLE® Pine-Passion-Banana Juice, chilled
1 tablespoon peach schnapps
1 tablespoon light rum
1 tablespoon orange liqueur
Cracked ice

• Pour juice, schnapps, rum and orange liqueur in 2 glasses. Add ice. Garnish as desired. *Makes 2 servings*

Fresh out of Harvard, Jim Dole arrived in Hawaii in 1899 and two years later began growing 60 acres of pineapple. Since fresh pineapple would not withstand long ocean voyages of that day, Dole had to build a cannery to pack the fruit. By 1905, the cannery was producing an amazing 25,000 cases of canned pineapple. In 1922, Dole purchased the entire Hawaiian island of Lanai and proceeded to build roads and tap underground water sources in order to grow, harvest and transport the delectable fruit.

Clockwise from top right: Raspberry Mint Cooler, Kokomo Quencher and Sunlight Sipper

"Lemon Float" Punch

**Juice of 10 to 12 SUNKIST® Lemons
    (2 cups)**
¾ cup sugar
4 cups water
1 bottle (2 liters) ginger ale, chilled
**1 pint lemon sherbet or frozen vanilla
    yogurt**
**Lemon half-cartwheel slices and
    fresh mint leaves (optional) for
    garnish**

Combine lemon juice and sugar; stir to
dissolve sugar. Add water; chill. To serve, in
large punch bowl, combine lemon mixture
and ginger ale. Add *small* scoops of sherbet,
lemon half-cartwheel slices and mint.

*Makes about 15 cups
(thirty 6-ounce servings)*

Oreo® Milk Shakes

18 OREO® Chocolate Sandwich Cookies
1½ pints vanilla ice cream, divided
1½ cups milk
¼ cup chocolate-flavored syrup

Coarsely chop 14 cookies. In electric blender
container, blend chopped cookies, 1 pint ice
cream, milk and chocolate syrup until well
blended and smooth, about 1 to 2 minutes.

Pour into 4 (8-ounce) glasses; top each with
scoop of remaining ice cream and cookie.

Makes 4 servings

Frozen Margaritas

1 cup confectioners' sugar
½ cup tequila
**⅓ cup REALIME® Lime Juice from
    Concentrate**
**¼ cup triple sec or other orange-
    flavored liqueur**
4 cups ice cubes

In blender container, combine all ingredients
except ice; blend well. Gradually add ice,
blending until smooth. Garnish as desired.
Serve immediately.   *Makes about 1 quart*

Bloody Mary Mix

4 cups vegetable juice cocktail
**2 tablespoons HEINZ® Worcestershire
    Sauce**
1 tablespoon fresh lime or lemon juice
¼ teaspoon granulated sugar
¼ teaspoon pepper
¼ teaspoon hot pepper sauce
⅛ teaspoon garlic powder

Thoroughly mix all ingredients; cover and
chill. Serve over ice. Garnish with celery
stalks and lime wedges, if desired.

Makes 4 servings

Note: To prepare Bloody Mary Cocktail, add
3 or 4 parts Bloody Mary Mix to 1 part vodka.

"Lemon Float" Punch

Simmering Soups & Stews

From soups and stews to chilis and gumbos, you'll have a souper selection to choose from on those chilly days when a big bowl of hot, hearty soup hits the spot.

Veg-All® Cheesy Chowder

¼ cup butter
1 medium onion, chopped
⅓ cup all-purpose flour
2 cups milk
1 (10¾-ounce) can chicken broth
1 package (8 ounces) pasteurized
    process cheese spread, cubed
¼ teaspoon hot pepper sauce
¼ teaspoon white pepper
1 (16-ounce) can VEG-ALL® Mixed
    Vegetables, drained
2 tablespoons chopped parsley

Melt butter in large saucepan. Add onion; cook until tender. Add flour, whisking until smooth. Cook 1 minute over low heat, stirring constantly. Gradually add milk and chicken broth; cook over medium heat, stirring constantly until thickened and bubbly. Add cheese and seasonings, stirring until cheese is melted. Add Veg-All® and parsley. Reduce heat and cook until thoroughly heated. *Do not boil.* *Makes 6 servings*

Veg-All® Cheesy Chowder

Cheddar Potato Chowder

3 tablespoons margarine or butter
2 medium-size carrots, peeled and diced
2 medium-size celery stalks, thinly sliced
1 small onion, chopped
3 tablespoons all-purpose flour
¼ teaspoon dry mustard
¼ teaspoon paprika
¼ teaspoon ground pepper
2 cups milk
2 cups water
4 medium-size IDAHO® Potatoes (about 1¾ pounds), peeled and cut into ½-inch cubes
2 chicken-flavor bouillon cubes or envelopes
1½ cups shredded Cheddar cheese
4 slices bacon, cooked and crumbled (optional)
Chopped chives (optional)

In 3-quart saucepan over medium heat, melt margarine. Add carrots, celery and onion; cook until tender, about 10 minutes, stirring occasionally. Stir in flour, dry mustard, paprika and pepper; cook 1 minute.

Gradually add milk, water, potatoes and bouillon. Bring to a boil over high heat; reduce heat to low. Cover and simmer 10 minutes or until potatoes are tender.

Remove saucepan from heat; add cheese and stir just until melted. Top each serving with crumbled bacon and chopped chives, if desired.   *Makes 4 servings*

Favorite recipe from **Idaho Potato Commission**

Idaho Potato Commission

All across the country, Idaho® Potatoes are the potatoes of choice for meals ranging from trendy to traditional. Because Idaho grows more potatoes than any other state, the Idaho Potato Commission is constantly searching the nation for the best Idaho Potato recipes.

Chicken Noodle Soup

1 (46-fluid ounce) can COLLEGE INN® Chicken Broth
½ pound boneless skinless chicken, cut into bite-size pieces
1½ cups uncooked medium egg noodles
1 cup sliced carrots
½ cup chopped onion
⅓ cup sliced celery
1 teaspoon dried dill weed
¼ teaspoon ground black pepper

In large saucepan, over medium-high heat, heat chicken broth, chicken, noodles, carrots, onion, celery, dill and pepper to a boil. Reduce heat; simmer 20 minutes or until chicken and noodles are cooked.
Makes 8 servings

In the 1920s, a chef named Joseph Colton saw opportunity knocking in the form of his popular recipe for chicken à la king. His delicious creation became a house specialty at the College Inn, a nightclub in the Sherman House in Chicago. Eventually, a small delicatessen was established at the hotel to handle the numerous take-home orders from patrons. Later, the Sherman House installed a cannery, and in 1923 the College Inn Food Products Corporation was born.

Seafood Bisque

½ **pound shrimp, shelled, deveined and cut in half crosswise**
½ **pound sea scallops, coarsely chopped**
1 **(16-ounce) can whole new potatoes, drained and diced**
1 **clove garlic, crushed**
¼ **cup margarine or butter**
⅔ **cup all-purpose flour**
2 **(13¾-fluid ounce) cans COLLEGE INN® Chicken Broth**
½ **teaspoon ground white pepper**
1 **cup light cream or half-and-half**

In large saucepan, over medium heat, cook shrimp, scallops, potatoes and garlic in margarine until seafood is done. Stir in flour until blended. Gradually add chicken broth and pepper. Heat to a boil, stirring constantly. Boil 1 minute. Stir in light cream; heat through. *Do not boil.*   *Makes 6 servings*

Hunt's® Hearty Manhattan Clam Chowder

2 **slices bacon, cut into ½-inch pieces**
½ **cup chopped onion**
½ **cup chopped celery**
1 **(14½-ounce) can HUNT'S® Whole Peeled Tomatoes, undrained and crushed**
1 **(14½-ounce) can HUNT'S® Whole New Potatoes, drained and cubed**
1 **(8-ounce) bottle clam juice**
1 **(6½-ounce) can chopped clams, drained and rinsed**
2 **tablespoons chopped fresh parsley**
¼ **teaspoon thyme**
⅛ **teaspoon pepper**
⅛ **teaspoon garlic powder**

In large saucepan, fry bacon until crisp. Add onion and celery; cook and stir until tender. Stir in tomatoes, potatoes, clam juice, clams, parsley, thyme, pepper and garlic powder. Simmer, uncovered, 15 minutes, stirring occasionally.   *Makes 4 servings*

Arizona Pork Chili

1½ pounds boneless pork, cut into
    ¼-inch cubes
1 tablespoon vegetable oil
1 onion, coarsely chopped
2 cloves garlic, minced
1 can (15 ounces) black, pinto or
    kidney beans, drained
1 can (14½ ounces) DEL MONTE® Chili
    Style Chunky Tomatoes
1 can (4 ounces) diced green chiles
1 teaspoon ground cumin

In large skillet, brown meat in oil over
medium-high heat. Add onion and garlic;
cook until onion is tender. Season with salt
and pepper, if desired. Add remaining
ingredients. Simmer 10 minutes, stirring
occasionally. Serve with tortillas and sour
cream, if desired. *Makes 6 servings*

Chili con Carne Winchester

2 tablespoons vegetable oil
⅓ cup chopped onion
⅓ cup chopped green bell pepper
1 pound ground beef
2 (15-ounce) cans kidney beans
1 (16-ounce) can stewed tomatoes
1 clove garlic, minced
1 (16-ounce) can VEG-ALL® Mixed
    Vegetables, undrained

1. Heat oil in 3-quart saucepan. Add onion
and green pepper; cook and stir over medium
heat until soft.

2. Add ground beef, drained kidney beans,
stewed tomatoes and garlic. Bring to a boil.
Cover and reduce heat; simmer 30 minutes.

3. Stir in undrained Veg-All® and cook 10
minutes longer. *Makes 6 servings*

Sock-It-To-'Em Chili

1 tablespoon vegetable oil
¾ pound ground turkey or lean ground
    beef
8 ounces mushrooms, sliced
2 medium carrots, peeled and diced
1 large green bell pepper, seeded and
    diced
1 medium onion, chopped
2 cloves garlic, minced
1½ teaspoons chili powder
½ teaspoon ground cumin
1 (26-ounce) jar NEWMAN'S OWN®
    Sockarooni™ Spaghetti Sauce
2 (15- to 19-ounce) cans black beans,
    undrained
1 cup water
1 medium zucchini, diced

In 5-quart Dutch oven over medium-high
heat, heat oil. Cook meat until no longer pink,
stirring constantly. Add mushrooms, carrots,
bell pepper, onion, garlic, chili powder and
cumin; cook, stirring frequently, until onion is
tender.

Stir in Newman's Own® Sockarooni™
Spaghetti Sauce, black beans with liquid and
water. Increase heat to high and bring to a
boil. Reduce heat to low; cover and simmer
20 minutes. Add zucchini; cook, uncovered,
over medium-low heat 10 minutes or until
zucchini is just tender. *Makes 6 servings*

Arizona Pork Chili

White Bean Stew

2½ quarts chicken stock *or* 5 cans
    (14½ ounces each) chicken broth
    plus ½ cup water
1 pound dried white beans
½ cup chopped onion
3 cloves garlic, minced
1 teaspoon LAWRY'S® Seasoned Salt
½ teaspoon LAWRY'S® Pinch of Herbs
½ teaspoon LAWRY'S® Lemon Pepper
5 boneless, skinless chicken breast
    halves (about 1 pound), cooked and
    diced
1 can (4 ounces) diced green chiles
2 teaspoons ground cumin
2 teaspoons dried oregano
2 teaspoons chopped cilantro
1 cup (4 ounces) shredded Cheddar
    cheese for garnish
¼ cup chopped green onions for
    garnish

In Dutch oven or large saucepan, combine
2 quarts chicken stock, beans, onion, garlic,
Seasoned Salt, Pinch of Herbs and Lemon
Pepper. Bring to a boil; reduce heat. Cover
and simmer until beans are tender, about
1½ hours. (If bean mixture becomes too
thick, add additional chicken stock to thin.)
When beans are tender, add remaining
ingredients except cheese and green onions;
cover and simmer 20 minutes, stirring
occasionally. Garnish as desired.

Makes 6 servings

Presentation: Serve stew in individual bowls.
Sprinkle with cheese and green onions.

Irish Stew in Bread

1½ pounds lean, boned American lamb
    shoulder, cut into 1-inch cubes
¼ cup all-purpose flour
2 tablespoons vegetable oil
2 cloves garlic, crushed
2 cups water
¼ cup Burgundy wine
5 medium carrots, chopped
3 medium potatoes, peeled and sliced
2 large onions, peeled and chopped
2 celery ribs, sliced
¾ teaspoon black pepper
1 beef bouillon cube, crushed
1 cup frozen peas
¼ pound fresh sliced mushrooms
    Round bread, unsliced*

*Stew may be served individually or in one large
loaf. Slice bread crosswise near top to form lid.
Hollow larger piece, leaving 1-inch border. Fill
"bowl" with hot stew; cover with "lid." Serve
immediately.

Coat lamb with flour while heating oil over
low heat in Dutch oven. Add lamb and garlic;
cook and stir until brown. Add water, wine,
carrots, potatoes, onions, celery, pepper and
bouillon. Cover; simmer 30 to 35 minutes.

Add peas and mushrooms. Cover; simmer 10
minutes. Bring to a boil; correct seasonings, if
necessary. Serve in bread.

Makes 6 to 8 servings

Favorite recipe from **American Lamb Council**

White Bean Stew

Tried & True One-Dish Classics

With these one-dish creations, preparing dinner will be lickety-split. Your family and friends will thank you and keep coming back for more.

Coq au Vin

4 thin slices bacon, cut into ½-inch pieces
6 chicken thighs, skinned
¾ teaspoon dried thyme, crushed
1 large onion, coarsely chopped
4 cloves garlic, minced
½ pound small red potatoes, quartered
10 mushrooms, quartered
1 can (14½ ounces) DEL MONTE® Italian Recipe Stewed Tomatoes
1½ cups dry red wine

In 4-quart heavy saucepan, cook bacon until just starting to brown. Sprinkle chicken with thyme; season with salt and pepper, if desired. Add chicken to pan; brown over medium-high heat. Add onion and garlic.

Cook 2 minutes; drain. Add potatoes, mushrooms, tomatoes and wine. Cook, uncovered, over medium-high heat about 25 minutes or until potatoes are tender and sauce thickens, stirring occasionally. Garnish with chopped parsley, if desired.

Makes 4 to 6 servings

Coq au Vin

Classic Arroz con Pollo

2 tablespoons olive oil
1 cut-up chicken
2 cups uncooked rice*
1 cup chopped onions
1 medium-size red bell pepper,
      chopped
1 medium-size green bell pepper,
      chopped
1 clove garlic, minced
1½ teaspoons salt, divided
1½ teaspoons dried basil
4 cups chicken broth
1 tablespoon lime juice
⅛ teaspoon ground saffron *or*
      ½ teaspoon ground turmeric
1 bay leaf
2 cups chopped tomatoes
½ teaspoon ground black pepper
1 cup fresh or frozen green peas
Fresh basil for garnish

*Recipe based on regular-milled long grain white rice.

Heat oil in large Dutch oven over medium-high heat until hot. Add chicken; cook 10 minutes or until brown, turning occasionally. Remove chicken; keep warm. Add rice, onions, bell peppers, garlic, ¾ teaspoon salt and dried basil to pan; cook and stir 5 minutes or until vegetables are tender and rice is browned. Add broth, lime juice, saffron and bay leaf. Bring to a boil; stir in tomatoes. Arrange chicken on top and sprinkle with remaining ¾ teaspoon salt and black pepper. Cover; reduce heat to low. Cook 20 minutes

more. Stir in peas; cover and cook 10 minutes more or until fork can be inserted into chicken with ease and juices run clear, not pink. Remove bay leaf. Garnish with fresh basil. Serve immediately.

Makes 8 servings

Favorite recipe from **National Broiler Council**

Easy Chicken Pot Pie

1¼ cups hot water
3 tablespoons PARKAY® Spread Sticks,
      cut into pieces
3 cups STOVE TOP® Stuffing Mix for
      Chicken in the Canister
1 can (10¾ ounces) condensed cream
      of chicken soup
1 cup milk
3 cups cooked chicken or turkey cubes
1 package (10 ounces) frozen mixed
      vegetables, thawed
1 can (4 ounces) sliced mushrooms,
      drained
¼ teaspoon dried thyme leaves

• Heat oven to 350°F.

• Mix hot water and spread in large bowl until margarine is melted. Stir in stuffing mix just to moisten; set aside.

• Mix soup and milk in another large bowl until smooth. Stir in chicken, vegetables, mushrooms and thyme. Pour into 12×8-inch glass baking dish. Spoon stuffing evenly over top.

• Bake 35 minutes or until heated through.

Makes 4 to 6 servings

Classic Arroz con Pollo

Almond-Chicken Casserole

1 cup fresh bread cubes
1 tablespoon margarine, melted
3 cups chopped cooked chicken
1½ cups diagonally cut celery slices
1 cup MIRACLE WHIP® Salad Dressing
1 cup (4 ounces) shredded 100%
**   Natural KRAFT® Swiss Cheese**
½ cup (1½-inch-long) red or green
**   pepper strips**
¼ cup slivered almonds, toasted
¼ cup chopped onion

• Combine bread cubes and margarine; toss lightly. Set aside. Combine remaining ingredients; mix lightly. Spoon into 10×6-inch baking dish. Top with bread cubes. Bake at 350°, 30 minutes or until lightly browned. Garnish as desired.   *Makes 6 servings*

Tuna Mac and Cheese

1 package (7¼ ounces) macaroni and
**   cheese dinner**
1 can (12 ounces) STARKIST® Solid
**   White or Chunk Light Tuna, drained**
**   and chunked**
1 cup frozen peas
½ cup shredded Cheddar cheese
½ cup milk
1 teaspoon Italian herb seasoning
¼ teaspoon garlic powder (optional)
1 tablespoon grated Parmesan cheese

Microwave Directions: Prepare macaroni and cheese dinner according to package directions. Add remaining ingredients except

Parmesan cheese. Pour into 1½-quart microwavable serving dish. Cover with vented plastic wrap; microwave on HIGH 2 minutes. Stir; continue heating on HIGH 2½ to 3½ more minutes or until cheese is melted and mixture is heated through. Sprinkle with Parmesan cheese.

Makes 5 to 6 servings

Classic Macaroni and Cheese

2 cups elbow macaroni
3 tablespoons butter or margarine
¼ cup chopped onion (optional)
2 tablespoons all-purpose flour
½ teaspoon salt
⅛ teaspoon pepper
2 cups milk
2 cups (8 ounces) SARGENTO® Classic
**   Supreme® or Fancy Supreme®**
**   Shredded Mild Cheddar Cheese,**
**   divided**

Cook macaroni according to package directions; drain. In medium saucepan, melt butter and cook onion about 5 minutes or until tender. Stir in flour, salt and pepper. Gradually add milk and cook, stirring occasionally, until thickened. Remove from heat. Add 1½ cups Cheddar cheese and stir until cheese melts. Combine cheese sauce with cooked macaroni. Place in 1½-quart casserole; top with remaining ½ cup Cheddar cheese. Bake at 350°F, 30 minutes or until bubbly and cheese is golden brown.

Makes 6 servings

Almond-Chicken Casserole

Family-Pleasing Meat Dishes

When it comes to the meat lovers in your household, look to this selection to give them a long list of meaty family favorites.

Beef with Dry Spice Rub

3 tablespoons firmly packed brown sugar
1 tablespoon black peppercorns
1 tablespoon yellow mustard seeds
1 tablespoon whole coriander seeds
4 cloves garlic
1½ to 2 pounds beef top round steak or London Broil (about 1½ inches thick)
Vegetable or olive oil
Salt

Place sugar, peppercorns, seeds and garlic in blender or food processor; process until seeds and garlic are crushed. Rub beef with oil, then pat on spice mixture. Season with salt. Oil hot grid to help prevent sticking. Grill beef, on covered grill, over medium-low KINGSFORD® briquets, 16 to 20 minutes for medium doneness, turning once. Let stand 5 minutes before slicing. Cut across grain into thin, diagonal slices. *Makes 6 servings*

Grilled Mushrooms: Thread mushrooms on metal or bamboo* skewers. Brush lightly with oil; season with salt and pepper. Grill 7 to 12 minutes, turning occasionally.

Grilled New Potatoes: Cook or microwave small new potatoes until barely tender. Thread on metal or bamboo* skewers. Brush lightly with oil; season with salt and pepper. Grill 10 to 15 minutes, turning occasionally.

*Bamboo skewers should be soaked in water at least 20 minutes to keep them from burning.

Top to bottom: Grilled New Potatoes, Grilled Mushrooms and Beef with Dry Spice Rub

Pronto Spicy Beef and Black Bean Salsa

1 beef tri-tip (bottom sirloin) roast or top sirloin steak, cut 1½ inches thick
1 can (15 ounces) black beans, rinsed, drained
1 medium tomato, chopped
1 small red onion, finely chopped
3 tablespoons coarsely chopped fresh cilantro
Fresh cilantro sprigs (optional)

Seasoning

1 tablespoon chili powder
1 teaspoon ground cumin
1 teaspoon salt
½ teaspoon ground red pepper

1. Combine seasoning ingredients; reserve 2 teaspoons for salsa. Trim fat from beef roast. Press remaining seasoning mixture evenly into surface of roast.

2. Place tri-tip on grid over medium coals (medium-low coals for top sirloin). Grill tri-tip 30 to 35 minutes (top sirloin 22 to 30 minutes) for rare to medium doneness, turning occasionally. Let stand 10 minutes before carving.

3. Meanwhile, in medium bowl, combine beans, tomato, onion, chopped cilantro and reserved seasoning mixture; mix until blended.

4. Carve roast across the grain into slices. Arrange beef and bean salsa on serving platter; garnish with cilantro sprigs, if desired.

Makes 6 servings

*Favorite recipe from **National Live Stock & Meat Board***

Country-Style Pot Roast

1 boneless pot roast (3 to 3½ pounds), rump, chuck or round
1 envelope LIPTON® Recipe Secrets® Onion-Mushroom Soup Mix
2½ cups water, divided
4 potatoes, cut into 1-inch pieces
4 carrots, thinly sliced
2 to 4 tablespoons all-purpose flour

In 5-quart Dutch oven or heavy saucepan, brown roast over medium-high heat. Add onion-mushroom soup mix blended with 2 cups water. Reduce heat to low and simmer covered, turning occasionally, 2 hours. Add vegetables and cook additional 30 minutes or until vegetables and roast are tender; remove roast and vegetables. Blend remaining ½ cup water with flour; stir into Dutch oven. Bring to a boil over high heat. Reduce heat to low and simmer, stirring constantly, until thickened, about 5 minutes.

Makes about 6 servings

Note: Also terrific with Lipton® Recipe Secrets® Onion, Beefy Onion or Italian Herb with Tomato Soup Mix.

Menu Suggestion: Serve with warm rolls and apple pie for dessert.

Pronto Spicy Beef and Black Bean Salsa

Grilled Meat Loaf and Potatoes

1 pound ground beef
½ cup A.1.® Steak Sauce
½ cup plain dry bread crumbs
1 egg
¼ cup finely chopped green bell pepper
¼ cup finely chopped onion
2 tablespoons margarine, melted
4 (6-ounce) red skin potatoes,
  parboiled and sliced into ¼-inch-
  thick rounds
Grated Parmesan cheese

In large bowl, combine ground beef, ¼ cup steak sauce, bread crumbs, egg, pepper and onion. Divide mixture and shape into 4 (4-inch) oval loaves. In small bowl, combine remaining ¼ cup steak sauce and margarine; set aside.

Over medium heat, grill meat loaves for 20 to 25 minutes and potato slices for 10 to 12 minutes, turning and brushing both occasionally with steak sauce mixture. Sprinkle potatoes with Parmesan cheese; serve immediately. *Makes 4 servings*

Souperior Meat Loaf

1 envelope LIPTON® Recipe Secrets®
  Onion Soup Mix
2 pounds ground beef
1½ cups fresh bread crumbs
2 eggs
¾ cup water
⅓ cup ketchup

Preheat oven to 350°F. In large bowl, combine all ingredients. In 13×9-inch baking or roasting pan, shape into loaf. Bake 1 hour or until done. Let stand 10 minutes before serving. *Makes about 8 servings*

Note: Also terrific with Lipton® Recipe Secrets® Beefy Onion, Onion-Mushroom, Italian Herb with Tomato or Savory Herb with Garlic Soup Mix.

The first sauce!
The finest sauce!
The best sauce of all!

BRAND'S A.I. *THE ORIGINAL THICK SAUCE*
A fine digestive & an excellent relish
BRAND & Co Ltd. MAYFAIR WORKS, VAUXHALL

A.1. Steak Sauce got its name when King George IV of England tasted it and proclaimed, "This is A-One."

Grilled Meat Loaf and Potatoes

Spareribs with Zesty Honey Sauce

1 cup chili sauce
½ to ¾ cup honey
¼ cup minced onion
2 tablespoons dry red wine (optional)
1 tablespoon Worcestershire sauce
1 teaspoon Dijon-style mustard
3 pounds pork spareribs
Salt and pepper

Combine chili sauce, honey, onion, wine, if desired, Worcestershire sauce and mustard in small saucepan. Cook and stir over medium heat until mixture comes to a boil. Reduce heat to low and simmer, uncovered, 5 minutes.

Sprinkle spareribs with salt and pepper. Place on rack in roasting pan; cover with foil. Roast at 375°F 35 to 45 minutes. Uncover and brush generously with sauce. Roast 45 minutes, brushing with sauce every 15 minutes, until spareribs are fully cooked and tender. Cut spareribs into serving portions and serve with remaining sauce.

Makes 4 servings

Favorite recipe from **National Honey Board**

Stuffed Pork Chops

4 rib pork chops, cut 1¼ inches thick,
slit for stuffing
1½ cups prepared stuffing
1 tablespoon vegetable oil
Salt and pepper
1 bottle (12 ounces) HEINZ® Chili Sauce

Trim excess fat from chops. Place stuffing in pockets of chops; secure with toothpicks. Brown chops in oil; season with salt and pepper. Place chops in 2-quart oblong baking dish. Pour chili sauce over chops. Cover dish with foil; bake in 350°F oven, 30 minutes. Stir sauce to blend; turn and baste chops. Cover; bake additional 30 to 40 minutes or until chops are tender. Remove toothpicks from chops. Skim excess fat from sauce.

Makes 4 servings

National Honey Board

The honey bee is the only insect that produces food eaten by man. Bees have been producing honey for 15 million years; man has harvested honey for three million years. Honey is also the only natural sweetener that needs no additional refining or processing to be utilized. Honey bees must tap two million flowers, flying over 55,000 miles, to make one pound of honey.

® © NHB

Spareribs with Zesty Honey Sauce

Chorizos with Onions à la Gonzalez

1 or 2 large Spanish onions sliced wafer thin to cover bottom of roasting pan
2 or 3 pounds CORTE'S® CHORIZOS*
1 or 2 bay leaves
½ cup dry white wine or wine and chicken broth combined to equal ½ cup

*Mexican sausage is available in the meat section of the supermarket.

Place onions in roasting pan. Cut chorizos diagonally into ⅜-inch pieces. Place over onions. Add bay leaves and wine. Bake at 375°F for 40 minutes or until crisp, turning once. Remove and discard bay leaves before serving.   *Makes 8 servings*

Honey Glazed Ham

¼ cup honey
3 tablespoons water
1½ teaspoons dry mustard
½ teaspoon ground ginger
¼ teaspoon ground cloves
1 fully cooked ham steak (about 12 to 16 ounces)
Fresh sage leaves for garnish (optional)

Combine honey, water and spices in small bowl. On top rack of preheated oven broiler, broil ham steak on both sides until lightly browned and thoroughly heated. Or, pan-fry ham steak on both sides in nonstick skillet over medium-high heat.

Place ham on heated serving dish; set aside. Add honey mixture to pan drippings and bring to a boil. Simmer 1 to 2 minutes, stirring. Brush sauce over ham; serve remaining sauce separately. Garnish with fresh sage leaves, if desired.   *Makes 4 servings*

*Favorite recipe from **National Honey Board***

Corte & Co.

Established in 1922, Corte & Co. manufactures Spanish and Portuguese sausages. Their chorizo sausages were developed for use in the kitchens of the Spanish Pavilion at the 1965 World's Fair in New York. Spicy or spicy hot, these smoked sausages have universal appeal for adding some zest to your favorite dish.

"EL BATURRO"®

Herb Crusted Racks of Lamb

Herb Crusted Racks of Lamb

2 racks of American lamb (8 ribs each), let stand at room temperature for 20 minutes*
1 cup finely chopped parsley
1 medium onion, finely chopped
1 tablespoon fresh dill weed, chopped, *or* 1 teaspoon dried dill weed
¼ cup fine dry bread crumbs
2 teaspoons fresh oregano leaves, chopped, *or* ½ teaspoon dried oregano
1 teaspoon salt
⅛ teaspoon ground pepper

*If lamb is roasted at refrigerator temperature, add 10 minutes to cooking time.

Preheat oven to 425°F. Combine all ingredients, except lamb; mix well. Pat mixture on outside of lamb.

Place on broiler rack in shallow roasting pan. Roast 30 minutes for medium rare.

Makes 4 servings

Note: Have butcher remove chine bone (back bone) and all excess fat.

*Favorite recipe from **American Lamb Council***

Pleasing Poultry Picks

Savor the exciting flavors of these chicken and turkey favorites. Fast, easy and versatile, these poultry selections are sure to spice up your dinner menus.

Chicken Morocco

1 cup uncooked bulgur wheat
4 chicken thighs, skinned
½ medium onion, chopped
1 tablespoon olive oil
1 can (14½ ounces) DEL MONTE®
    Original Recipe Stewed Tomatoes
    (No Salt Added)
½ cup DEL MONTE® Prune Juice
6 DEL MONTE® Pitted Prunes, diced
¼ teaspoon ground allspice

In large saucepan, bring 1½ cups water to boil; add bulgur. Cover and cook over low heat 20 minutes or until tender. Meanwhile, season chicken with salt-free herb seasoning, if desired. In large skillet, brown chicken with onion in oil over medium-high heat; drain. Stir in tomatoes, prune juice, prunes and allspice. Cover and cook 10 minutes over medium heat.

Remove cover; cook over medium-high heat 10 to 12 minutes or until sauce thickens and chicken is no longer pink, turning chicken and stirring sauce occasionally. Serve chicken and sauce over bulgur. Garnish with chopped parsley, if desired. *Makes 4 servings*

Chicken Morocco

Stuffed Chicken with Apple Glaze

1 broiler-fryer chicken (3½ to 4 pounds)
½ teaspoon salt
¼ teaspoon pepper
2 tablespoons vegetable oil
1 package (6 ounces) chicken-flavored stuffing mix plus ingredients to prepare mix
1 cup chopped apple
¼ cup chopped walnuts
¼ cup raisins
¼ cup thinly sliced celery
½ teaspoon grated lemon peel
½ cup apple jelly
1 tablespoon lemon juice
½ teaspoon ground cinnamon

Preheat oven to 350°F. Sprinkle inside of chicken with salt and pepper; rub outside with oil. Prepare stuffing mix in large bowl according to package directions. Add apple, walnuts, raisins, celery and lemon peel; mix thoroughly. Stuff body cavity loosely with stuffing.* Place chicken in baking pan. Cover loosely with aluminum foil; roast 1 hour. Meanwhile, combine jelly, lemon juice and cinnamon in small saucepan. Simmer over low heat 3 minutes or until blended. Remove foil from chicken; brush with glaze. Roast chicken, uncovered, brushing frequently with glaze, 30 minutes or until meat thermometer inserted into thickest part of thigh registers 185°F and juices run clear. Let chicken stand 15 minutes before carving.

Makes 4 servings

*Bake any leftover stuffing in covered casserole alongside chicken until heated through.

*Favorite recipe from **Delmarva Poultry Industry, Inc.***

Oven Tender Chicken™

1 broiler-fryer chicken, cut up (3 to 3½ pounds)
1 (18-ounce) bottle KRAFT® Original Barbecue Sauce

• Heat oven to 350°F.

• Place chicken in 13×9-inch baking dish. Pour barbecue sauce over chicken. Bake, uncovered, 1 hour or until cooked through.

Makes 4 servings

Double-Coated Chicken

7 cups KELLOGG'S® CORN FLAKES® cereal, crushed to 1¾ cups
1 egg
1 cup skim milk
1 cup all-purpose flour
½ teaspoon salt
¼ teaspoon black pepper
3 pounds broiler chicken pieces, washed and patted dry
3 tablespoons margarine, melted

1. Measure crushed Kellogg's® Corn Flakes® cereal into shallow dish or pan. Set aside.

2. In small mixing bowl, beat egg and milk until combined. Add flour, salt and pepper. Mix until smooth. Dip chicken in batter. Coat with cereal. Place in single layer, skin side up, in foil-lined shallow baking pan. Drizzle with margarine.

3. Bake at 350°F about 1 hour or until chicken is tender. *Do not cover pan or turn chicken while baking.*   *Makes 8 servings*

Stuffed Chicken with Apple Glaze

Magically Moist Chicken

1 chicken (2½ to 3½ pounds), cut into pieces
½ cup HELLMANN'S® or BEST FOODS® Real or Light Mayonnaise or Low Fat Mayonnaise Dressing
1¼ cups Italian seasoned bread crumbs

Brush chicken on all sides with mayonnaise. Place bread crumbs in large plastic food storage bag. Add chicken 1 piece at a time; shake to coat well. Arrange on rack in broiler pan. Bake in 425°F oven about 40 minutes or until golden brown and tender.

Makes 4 servings

Creole Chicken Thighs

8 skinless broiler-fryer chicken thighs
2 tablespoons butter or margarine
½ pound mushrooms, sliced
1 medium onion, chopped
½ cup chopped green bell pepper
½ cup thinly sliced celery
2 cloves garlic, minced
1 can (16 ounces) tomatoes, cut up
½ teaspoon salt
½ teaspoon sugar
½ teaspoon dried thyme leaves, crumbled
½ teaspoon hot pepper sauce
2 bay leaves
2 cups hot cooked rice

In skillet, melt butter over medium-high heat. Add mushrooms, onion, bell pepper, celery and garlic. Cook, stirring constantly, about 3 minutes or until onion is translucent, but not brown. Stir in tomatoes, salt, sugar, thyme, pepper sauce and bay leaves. Add chicken, spooning sauce over chicken. Cook, covered, over medium heat 35 minutes or until chicken is tender and juices run clear. Remove and discard bay leaves. Serve chicken and sauce over rice.

Makes 4 servings

*Favorite recipe from **Delmarva Poultry Industry, Inc.***

Lemon Herbed Chicken

½ cup butter or margarine
½ cup vegetable oil
⅓ cup lemon juice
2 tablespoons finely chopped parsley
2 tablespoons garlic salt
1 teaspoon dried rosemary, crushed
1 teaspoon dried summer savory, crushed
½ teaspoon dried thyme, crushed
¼ teaspoon coarsely cracked black pepper
6 chicken quarters (breast-wing or thigh-drumstick combinations)

Combine butter, oil, lemon juice, parsley, garlic salt, rosemary, summer savory, thyme and pepper in small saucepan. Heat until butter melts. Place chicken in shallow glass dish. Brush with some of sauce. Let stand 10 to 15 minutes. Oil hot grid to help prevent sticking. Place dark meat pieces on grill 10 minutes before white meat pieces (dark meat takes longer to cook). Grill chicken, on uncovered grill, over medium-hot KINGSFORD® briquets, 30 to 45 minutes for breast quarters or 50 to 60 minutes for leg quarters. Chicken is done when meat is no longer pink by bone. Turn quarters over and baste with sauce every 10 minutes.

Makes 6 servings

In 1911, Procter & Gamble began producing Crisco®. Following the introduction, home economists traveled the country touting Crisco® as the latest invention for the modern homemaker.

Classic Fried Chicken

¾ **cup all-purpose flour**
1 **teaspoon salt**
¼ **teaspoon pepper**
1 **frying chicken (2½ to 3 pounds), cut up or chicken pieces**
½ **cup CRISCO® all-vegetable shortening or ½ CRISCO® Stick**

1. **Combine** flour, salt and pepper in paper or plastic bag. **Add** a few pieces of chicken at a time. **Shake** to coat.

2. **Heat** shortening to 365°F in electric skillet or on medium-high heat in large heavy skillet. **Fry** chicken 30 to 40 minutes without lowering heat. **Turn** once for even browning. **Drain** on paper towels.   *Makes 4 servings*

Herb Garlic Grilled Chicken

¼ **cup chopped parsley**
1½ **tablespoons minced garlic**
4 **teaspoons grated lemon peel**
1 **tablespoon chopped fresh mint**
1 **chicken (2½ to 3 pounds), quartered**

Combine parsley, garlic, lemon peel and mint. Loosen skin from breast and thigh portions of chicken quarters by running fingers between skin and meat. Rub some of seasoning mixture evenly over meat under skin, then replace skin and rub remaining seasonings over outside of chicken to cover evenly. Arrange medium-hot KINGSFORD® briquets on one side of covered grill. Place chicken on grid opposite coals. Cover grill and cook chicken 45 to 55 minutes, turning once or twice. Chicken is done when juices run clear.
Makes 4 servings

Country Herb Roasted Chicken

1 chicken (2½ to 3 pounds), cut into serving pieces (with or without skin) *or* 1½ pounds boneless skinless chicken breast halves
1 envelope LIPTON® Recipe Secrets® Savory Herb with Garlic or Golden Herb with Lemon Soup Mix
2 tablespoons water
1 tablespoon olive or vegetable oil

Preheat oven to 375°F.

In 13×9-inch baking or roasting pan, arrange chicken. In small bowl, combine remaining ingredients; brush on chicken.

For *chicken pieces,* bake uncovered 45 minutes or until chicken is no longer pink. For *chicken breast halves,* bake uncovered 20 minutes or until chicken is no longer pink.

Makes about 4 servings

Baked Chicken with Red-Peppered Onions

1 broiler-fryer chicken, quartered
2 teaspoons lemon pepper seasoning
1 teaspoon olive oil
4 cups thinly sliced sweet onions
4 tablespoons red hot pepper jelly
1 small sweet red pepper, cut into rings
Cilantro

On oiled rack of large broiler pan, place chicken. Sprinkle chicken with lemon pepper seasoning. Bake in 400°F oven, skin side up, 50 minutes or until chicken is fork-tender.

Meanwhile, add olive oil to large nonstick skillet; heat to medium temperature. Add onions; cook until barely wilted, about 5 minutes. Add jelly and stir gently until melted. Spoon half of onion mixture on large platter. Arrange chicken over onions; top with remaining onions. Garnish with pepper rings and cilantro.

Makes 4 servings

*Favorite recipe from **Delmarva Poultry Industry, Inc.***

Hunter-Style Chicken

4 slices bacon, cut into 1-inch pieces
1 medium onion, sliced
1 tablespoon vegetable oil
2 to 2½ pounds broiler-fryer pieces
1 can (16 ounces) tomatoes, cut into bite-size pieces
⅓ cup HEINZ® 57 Sauce
⅛ teaspoon pepper
Hot cooked rice or noodles

In large skillet, cook and stir bacon until crisp. Remove bacon; drain fat. Cook and stir onion in oil until tender; remove. In same skillet, brown chicken adding more oil if necessary. Drain excess fat. Combine bacon, onion, tomatoes, 57 Sauce and pepper; pour over chicken. Cover; simmer 20 to 25 minutes or until chicken is tender, basting occasionally. Remove chicken. Skim excess fat from sauce. If thicker sauce is desired, gradually stir in mixture of equal parts flour and water, simmering until thickened. Serve chicken and sauce with rice or noodles.

Makes 4 to 5 servings

Country Herb Roasted Chicken

Tarragon Chicken with Asparagus

¼ cup instant minced onion
1 tablespoon vegetable oil
1 pound fresh asparagus, cut into
     1-inch pieces (about 3 cups)
1¼ cups diced red bell pepper
12 ounces boneless skinless chicken
     breasts, cut into 1-inch pieces
1¼ cups orange juice, divided
1 teaspoon cornstarch
1 teaspoon dried tarragon leaves,
     crushed
¼ teaspoon salt
⅛ teaspoon ground black pepper
     Hot cooked fettuccine

In small cup combine onion and ¼ cup water; set aside for 10 minutes to soften. In large nonstick skillet over medium-high heat, heat oil until hot. Add asparagus and red pepper; cook, stirring constantly, until nearly crisp-tender, about 3 minutes.

Add chicken and reserved onion mixture; cook, stirring constantly, until chicken is opaque, about 2 minutes. In small bowl combine ¼ cup orange juice and cornstarch; mix until smooth. Stir orange juice mixture into skillet along with remaining 1 cup orange juice, tarragon, salt and black pepper; cook, stirring constantly, until mixture thickens and boils, 2 to 3 minutes. Boil, stirring constantly, 1 minute longer.

Serve over hot cooked fettuccine and garnish with orange slices, if desired.

Makes 4 servings

Favorite recipe from **American Spice Trade Association**

Chicken Breasts Diavolo

6 chicken breast halves, boned,
     skinned and slightly flattened
½ cup finely minced fresh parsley
1 teaspoon lemon pepper seasoning
     Dash salt
     Dash garlic powder
3 tablespoons olive oil
3 (6-ounce) jars marinated artichoke
     hearts
1 tablespoon fresh lemon juice
1 (26-ounce) jar NEWMAN'S OWN®
     Diavolo Sauce
½ cup red wine (preferably Chianti)
1½ cups shredded mozzarella cheese
1½ cups onion-garlic flavor croutons
     (tossed with 1 tablespoon olive oil)
6 cups hot cooked pasta or rice

Preheat oven to 350°F. Sprinkle chicken breasts with parsley, lemon pepper seasoning, salt and garlic powder. Roll each breast, seasoned side in; secure with wooden toothpicks. Cook and stir in olive oil in large skillet until golden brown. Remove from pan with tongs and place in 13×9-inch baking dish. Carefully remove toothpicks.

Drain artichoke hearts; sprinkle with lemon juice and distribute among rolled chicken breasts.

Combine Newman's Own® Diavolo Sauce with wine; pour over chicken and artichokes. Sprinkle cheese evenly over top. Sprinkle with crouton mixture. Bake 30 to 40 minutes until golden brown and bubbly.

Spoon chicken over pasta or rice. Serve with crusty Italian bread or rolls, a green salad and remaining red wine.

Makes 6 servings

Chicken Marsala

4 boneless, skinless chicken breasts
   Salt and pepper to taste
¼ cup all-purpose flour
2 tablespoons WESSON® Oil
3 cups sliced mushrooms
1 cup sliced onions
1 teaspoon minced garlic
1 (15-ounce) can HUNT'S® Ready
   Tomato Sauces Chunky Special
⅓ cup Marsala wine
½ teaspoon salt
¼ teaspoon sugar

Season chicken with salt and pepper; coat lightly with flour. In large skillet, in hot oil, lightly brown chicken on both sides; remove and set aside. Add mushrooms, onions and garlic to skillet; cook and stir until tender. Stir in remaining ingredients. Return chicken to skillet; spoon sauce over to coat. Simmer, covered, 15 minutes.   *Makes 4 servings*

Simple Marinated Chicken Breasts

2 teaspoons Dijon mustard
1 clove garlic, minced
½ teaspoon salt
½ teaspoon ground black pepper
⅛ teaspoon dried savory
⅛ teaspoon dried tarragon
2 tablespoons olive oil, divided
¼ cup dry white wine
4 boneless, skinless chicken breast
   halves (about 1½ pounds)
½ cup warm water
   Fresh thyme for garnish

Combine mustard, garlic, salt, pepper, savory, tarragon, 1 tablespoon oil and wine in small bowl. Place chicken in shallow dish; pour mixture over chicken, turning to coat. Cover; marinate in refrigerator overnight.

Heat remaining 1 tablespoon oil in large skillet over medium heat until hot. Add chicken, reserving marinade; cook 15 minutes or until brown and no longer pink in center, turning occasionally. Remove to warm platter. Place marinade and warm water in skillet. Bring to a boil; cook and stir about 3 minutes. Pour over chicken. Garnish with thyme. Serve immediately.

Makes 4 servings

*Favorite recipe from **National Broiler Council***

NBC
National Broiler Council

The National Broiler Council is the nonprofit trade organization for the broiler chicken industry. Membership includes broiler producers and processors, firms that supply goods and services to the broiler industry and other companies involved in the industry. Members produce, process and market over 90% of all U.S. broilers. The Council is located in Washington, D.C., and is the primary source of information concerning the production, marketing and use of chicken.

Skillet Chicken Vesuvio

- 1 package (6.9 ounces) RICE-A-RONI® Chicken Flavor
- 12 unpeeled garlic cloves
- 3 tablespoons olive oil or vegetable oil
- 1½ teaspoons dried oregano leaves
- ½ teaspoon salt (optional)
- ½ teaspoon freshly ground black pepper
- ¼ teaspoon dried rosemary leaves (optional)
- 4 skinless, boneless chicken breast halves
- 1 medium tomato, chopped
- 4 lemon wedges (optional)

1. Prepare Rice-A-Roni® Mix as package directs.

2. While Rice-A-Roni® is simmering, combine garlic cloves and oil in second large skillet. Cover; cook over medium heat 5 minutes.

3. Combine seasonings; sprinkle over chicken.

4. Push garlic to edge of skillet. Add chicken; cook about 5 minutes on each side or until chicken is no longer pink inside. Remove garlic with slotted spoon. Squeeze softened garlic over chicken; discard garlic peels.

5. Stir tomato into rice. Serve rice topped with chicken, juices and lemon wedges.
Makes 4 servings

Stuffed Turkey Breasts

- 2 skinned and boned turkey breast halves* (about ¾ pound each)
- ¼ cup dry bread crumbs
- 1 tablespoon dried basil, crushed, *or* 3 tablespoons chopped fresh basil
- 1 teaspoon seasoned salt, divided Pepper to taste
- 1 can (16 ounces) USA Bartlett pear halves or slices
- 1 can (4 ounces) whole pimiento
- 1 tablespoon olive oil
- ½ cup dry white wine
- 1 teaspoon lemon juice

*One large turkey breast (about 1½ pounds) may be used.

Spread turkey breasts on cutting board. If necessary, pound with meat tenderizer to even thickness. Combine bread crumbs, basil, ½ teaspoon seasoned salt and pepper. Drain pears reserving ¼ cup pear liquid. If using pear halves, slice each into thirds. Layer pimiento, pears and crumb mixture on turkey. Roll up and tie or fasten with skewers or wooden picks. Place in oiled baking dish; brush with oil and sprinkle with remaining ½ teaspoon seasoned salt. Bake at 375°F, 30 minutes or until juices run clear. Transfer drippings to small saucepan; add wine and reserved pear liquid. Boil mixture until reduced by half. Add lemon juice and adjust seasonings. Slice turkey; spoon sauce over slices.
Makes 4 servings

*Favorite recipe from **Canned Fruit Promotion Service, Inc.***

Skillet Chicken Vesuvio

Curried Turkey with Pear Chutney

¼ cup chutney
⅓ cup chopped pear (about ½ pear)
2 teaspoons cider vinegar or wine vinegar
1 teaspoon canola oil or walnut oil
¼ cup (1 ounce) chopped California walnuts
5 to 6 teaspoons curry powder, divided
1 tablespoon unsalted butter
1 tablespoon canola oil
1 onion, sliced
¼ cup all-purpose flour
2 cups no-salt-added chicken broth
1 cup nonfat milk
   Salt and pepper (optional)
1 pound cooked turkey breast meat, cut into 1-inch cubes
2 cups cooked rice

Combine chutney, pear and vinegar; cover and chill until serving.

Heat 1 teaspoon oil in medium skillet. Add nuts; toss 3 to 4 minutes until lightly toasted. Sprinkle with 1 teaspoon curry powder; toss to combine. Set aside to cool.

Heat butter and 1 tablespoon oil in large saucepan. Add remaining 4 to 5 teaspoons curry powder; cook 1 minute. Add onion; cook about 5 minutes. Add flour and cook, stirring constantly, 2 minutes longer. Add chicken broth and milk; whisk until smooth. Bring to a boil; season with salt and pepper, if desired. Add turkey; simmer until heated through. Serve over rice, with sides of chutney and curried walnuts.

Makes about 4 servings

*Favorite recipe from **Walnut Marketing Board***

Busy Day Turkey Loaf

1 cup KELLOGG'S® CROUTETTES® Stuffing Mix
½ cup skim milk
2 egg whites
2 teaspoons Worcestershire sauce
¼ cup finely chopped onion
½ teaspoon salt
1 pound lean ground turkey
¼ cup ketchup
1 teaspoon prepared mustard
2 teaspoons brown sugar

1. Combine Kellogg's® Croutettes® Stuffing Mix and milk in large mixing bowl. Let stand 5 minutes or until Croutettes are softened.

2. Add egg whites, Worcestershire sauce, onion and salt. Beat well. Add ground turkey. Mix until well combined.

3. Shape into loaf. Place in foil-lined shallow baking pan. Score loaf by making several diagonal grooves across top.

4. Stir together ketchup, mustard and sugar. Fill grooves with ketchup mixture.

5. Bake at 350°F about 45 minutes or until browned.
Makes 6 servings

Curried Turkey with Pear Chutney

Treasures from the Sea

Enjoy the wonders of the sea with these time-tested treasures. This spectacular collection of fish and shellfish recipes is sure to delight the entire crew.

Albacore Stir-Fry

3 tablespoons vegetable oil
½ cup sliced onion
1 clove garlic, minced or pressed
1 bag (16 ounces) frozen Oriental vegetables, thawed and drained*
1 can (12 ounces) STARKIST® Solid White Tuna, drained and chunked
3 tablespoons soy sauce
1 tablespoon lemon juice
1 tablespoon water
1 teaspoon sugar
2 cups hot cooked rice

*May use 4 cups fresh vegetables, such as carrots, peapods, broccoli, bell peppers, mushrooms, celery and bean sprouts.

In wok or large skillet, heat oil over medium-high heat; sauté onion and garlic until onion is soft. Add vegetables; cook about 3 to 4 minutes or until vegetables are crisp-tender. Add tuna, soy sauce, lemon juice, water and sugar. Cook 1 more minute; serve over rice.

Makes 4 servings

Albacore Stir-Fry

Company's Coming Fish Roll-Ups

1 tablespoon margarine
2 tablespoons flour
¼ teaspoon paprika
⅛ teaspoon salt
1¼ cups lowfat milk
¾ cup shredded reduced fat Cheddar cheese, divided
6 cups (10-ounce package or 1-pound bunch) fresh spinach leaves, coarsely chopped, cooked and well drained
2 tablespoons thinly sliced green onion
6 sole, haddock or flounder fillets (about 1½ pounds)
Grated peel and juice of ½ SUNKIST® Lemon
3 cups hot cooked rice
Lemon cartwheel twists or wedges

For cheese sauce, in small saucepan, melt margarine; remove from heat. Stir in flour, paprika and salt; gradually stir in milk. Cook over medium heat, stirring until thickened; remove from heat. Stir in ½ cup cheese. In large bowl, add ⅓ cup cheese sauce to spinach and green onion; blend well. Sprinkle both sides of fish fillets with lemon juice. Divide spinach mixture on fillets; roll up. Place seam side down in 9-inch baking dish. Sprinkle roll-ups with lemon peel. Spoon remaining cheese sauce over fish roll-ups. Bake in preheated 350°F oven 30 to 35 minutes or until fish flakes easily with fork. Sprinkle with remaining ¼ cup cheese; bake until cheese melts. Garnish with additional sliced green onion, if desired. Serve each roll-up with ½ cup hot rice. Stir remaining sauce; serve over fish and rice. Garnish with lemon cartwheel twists or wedges.
Makes 6 servings

Festive Baked Stuffed Fish

4 tablespoons butter or margarine
2 teaspoons DILIJAN® Liquid Spice Dill
1½ teaspoons DILIJAN® Liquid Spice Garlic
½ cup chopped celery
½ cup chopped red bell pepper
¼ cup chopped shallots
¼ pound shiitake mushrooms, sliced
6 slices KAVLI® Hearty Thick Crispbread, crumbled
1 cup diced JARLSBERG LITE™ Cheese
1 tablespoon chopped parsley
8 flounder fillets (about 1 pound)
8 salmon fillets (about 1 pound)
Salt and pepper to taste
Additional chopped parsley

Melt butter in medium skillet. Add Liquid Dill and Garlic. Add celery, bell pepper, shallots and mushrooms; cook 8 to 10 minutes or until tender but not browned. Stir in crispbread crumbs, cheese and 1 tablespoon parsley. Spoon into 11×8×1½-inch ovenproof shallow baking dish.

Preheat oven to 350°F. Season fillets with salt and pepper. Fold fillets in halves or thirds and arrange over cheese stuffing in baking dish, alternating for braid effect. Cover loosely with foil. Bake 20 to 25 minutes or until fish flakes easily when tested with fork and cheese is melted. Sprinkle with additional parsley.
Makes 8 servings

Company's Coming Fish Roll-Ups

Seafood Kabobs

Seafood Kabobs

1 medium avocado
⅓ cup pineapple juice
⅓ cup REALEMON® Lemon Juice from
    Concentrate or REALIME® Lime
    Juice from Concentrate
2 tablespoons vegetable oil
1 to 2 tablespoons brown sugar
1 teaspoon grated orange rind
¼ teaspoon ground cinnamon
¾ pound large raw shrimp, peeled and
    deveined
½ pound sea scallops
1 cup melon chunks or balls

Peel and seed avocado; cut into chunks. In large shallow dish or plastic bag, combine juices, oil, sugar, orange rind and cinnamon; mix well. Add seafood and melon. Cover; marinate in refrigerator 4 hours or overnight. Remove seafood and melon from marinade; heat marinade thoroughly. Alternately thread shrimp, scallops, melon and avocado on skewers. Grill or broil 3 to 6 minutes or until shrimp are pink and scallops are opaque, basting frequently with marinade. Refrigerate leftovers. *Makes 4 servings*

Blue Diamond Growers

During World War II, the demand for almonds increased greatly in order to supply the Armed Forces with the popular chocolate and almond candy bars.

Trout Almondine

    2 tablespoons flour
 1½ teaspoons salt, divided
    ¼ teaspoon pepper
    2 pounds trout or fish fillets
    6 tablespoons butter or margarine,
        divided
    ¼ cup BLUE DIAMOND® Blanched
        Slivered Almonds
    3 tablespoons lemon juice*
    1 tablespoon chopped parsley

*If desired, reduce lemon juice to 1 teaspoon and add ¼ cup sherry or sauterne wine.

Mix flour, 1 teaspoon salt and pepper; sprinkle on fish. In skillet, over medium heat, fry fish in 4 tablespoons butter about 6 minutes or until lightly browned. Arrange fish on warmed platter. Add remaining butter to skillet and brown almonds lightly, stirring as needed. Stir in remaining salt, lemon juice and parsley; pour over fish. Serve immediately.   *Makes 4 to 6 servings*

Shrimp Curry

    2 pounds raw medium or large shrimp,
        peeled and deveined
    1 cup chopped onions
    ¼ cup margarine or butter
    ¼ cup unsifted flour
 2½ cups BORDEN® or MEADOW GOLD®
        Milk or Half-and-Half
    ¾ cup COCO LOPEZ® Cream of
        Coconut
    1 tablespoon curry powder
    1 teaspoon salt
    ½ teaspoon ground ginger
    ¼ cup REALEMON® Lemon Juice from
        Concentrate or REALIME® Lime
        Juice from Concentrate
    Hot cooked rice

In large skillet, cook and stir onions in margarine until tender; stir in flour. Gradually add milk; stir until smooth. Add cream of coconut, curry, salt and ginger. Over medium heat, cook and stir until thickened. Add ReaLemon® brand. Reduce heat; simmer uncovered 20 minutes, stirring occasionally. Add shrimp. Over medium heat, cook 5 to 10 minutes, stirring occasionally, until shrimp are opaque. Serve over rice with condiments. Refrigerate leftovers.

Makes 6 to 8 servings

Condiments: Toasted coconut, sunflower meats, chopped peanuts, sliced green onion, chopped hard-cooked eggs, chutney, crumbled bacon or raisins.

New West Crab Cakes

1 pound crabmeat
2 egg whites
1 egg yolk
**¾ pound Idaho potatoes, mashed (or
    1 cup instant mashed potatoes)**
⅓ cup chopped red onion or chives
**½ cup chopped California Walnuts,
    divided**
1 cup bread crumbs, divided
Pinch of salt

Combine crabmeat, egg whites, egg yolk, potatoes, onion, ¼ cup chopped walnuts, ½ cup bread crumbs and salt in medium bowl. Form into 8 flat patties. Mix together remaining ½ cup bread crumbs and ¼ cup finely chopped walnuts. Coat crab patties with bread crumb mixture. Cook over medium heat in skillet brushed with oil.

Serve with lemon wedges, fresh tomato relish or prepared salsa.   *Makes 4 servings*

*Favorite recipe from **Walnut Marketing Board***

Hot Crab Melt

**1 (6-ounce) can HARRIS® or ORLEANS®
    Crab Meat, drained**
**¼ cup BENNETT'S® Cocktail or Tartar
    Sauce**
2 tablespoons finely chopped celery
**2 tablespoons finely chopped green
    bell pepper**
2 English muffins, split and toasted
**4 slices BORDEN® Process American
    Cheese Food**

Preheat oven to 350°F. In small bowl, combine crab meat, sauce, celery and green pepper; spread equal amounts on muffin halves. Bake 5 minutes. Top each with cheese food slice; bake 5 minutes longer or until melted. Serve immediately. Refrigerate leftovers.   *Makes 4 servings*

White Clam Sauce

2 cloves garlic, finely chopped
¼ cup olive oil
**2 (6½-ounce) cans DOXSEE® or
    SNOW'S® Minced or Chopped
    Clams, drained, reserving liquid**
**1 (8-ounce) bottle DOXSEE® or
    SNOW'S® Clam Juice**
1 tablespoon chopped parsley
¼ teaspoon basil leaves
Dash pepper

In medium saucepan, cook garlic in oil until tender. Add reserved clam liquid, clam juice, parsley, basil and pepper. Bring to a boil. Reduce heat; simmer 5 minutes. Add clams; heat through. Serve over hot cooked CREAMETTE® Linguine topped with grated Parmesan cheese. Refrigerate leftovers.
Makes about 2½ cups

Heinz® factory workers hand peeling tomatoes in 1910.

Seafood Cocktail Sauce

1 cup **HEINZ®** Chili Sauce
1 tablespoon prepared horseradish
1 teaspoon lemon juice*
 Hot pepper sauce to taste

*One teaspoon Heinz® Vinegar may be substituted.

Combine chili sauce, horseradish, lemon juice and hot pepper sauce. Serve with chilled shrimp, seafood, broiled fish or fish sticks. *Makes about 1 cup*

Pasta
Mania &
More

Not just spaghetti anymore!
The versatility of pasta is apparent
with these taste-tempting sensations
for all occasions.

Rigatoni with Creamy Tomato Sauce

8 ounces dry pasta (rigatoni or penne), cooked, drained and kept warm
1 tablespoon olive oil
½ cup diced onion
2 tablespoons dry vermouth or white wine
1¾ cups (14.5-ounce can) CONTADINA® Pasta Ready™ Chunky Tomatoes, Primavera
½ cup heavy cream
1 cup California Ripe Olives, halved
½ cup grated Parmesan cheese
¼ cup sliced green onions

In large skillet, heat oil; add onion and sauté 4 to 5 minutes. Add vermouth; cook 1 minute. Stir in tomatoes and juice, cream, pasta, olives and Parmesan cheese; toss well. Sprinkle with green onions.

Makes 4 servings

Rigatoni with Creamy Tomato Sauce

Hunt's® Linguine with Red Clam Sauce

  1 tablespoon olive oil
  ¾ cup finely chopped onion
  ½ teaspoon fresh minced garlic
  1 (15-ounce) can HUNT'S® Tomato
    Sauce
  1 (10-ounce) can whole baby clams,
    reserve ¼ cup clam juice
  1 tablespoon chopped fresh parsley
  1 teaspoon crushed basil
  ½ teaspoon crushed oregano
  ⅛ teaspoon pepper
  ¾ pound linguine, cooked and drained
    Grated Parmesan cheese

In large saucepan, heat oil; sauté onion and garlic until tender. Stir in tomato sauce, clams, clam juice, parsley, basil, oregano and pepper. Simmer, uncovered, for 10 to 15 minutes; stir occasionally. Serve over linguine and top with Parmesan cheese.

Makes 4 servings

Four-Pepper Penne

  1 medium onion, sliced
  1 small red bell pepper, thinly sliced
  1 small green bell pepper, thinly sliced
  1 small yellow bell pepper, thinly sliced
1½ teaspoons minced garlic
  1 tablespoon vegetable oil
  1 (26-ounce) jar HEALTHY CHOICE®
    Traditional Pasta Sauce
  1 teaspoon dried basil
  ½ teaspoon dried savory
  ¼ teaspoon black pepper
  ½ pound penne, cooked and drained

In Dutch oven or large nonstick saucepan, cook and stir onion, bell peppers and garlic in hot oil until vegetables are tender-crisp. Add pasta sauce, basil, savory and black pepper. Heat through over medium heat. Serve over penne.

Makes 6 servings

HEALTHY CHOICE *Healthy Choice® introduced its first products, frozen dinners, in 1988. Today, Healthy Choice offers consumers more than 300 products that are found in nearly every section of the grocery store. Products include frozen meals, cold cuts, franks, smoked sausages, service deli meats, pasta sauces, fat-free cheese, ready-to-serve soup, premium low-fat ice cream and multi grain cereal. All Healthy Choice products contain less than 30 percent of calories from total fat and less than 10 percent of calories from saturated fat.*

Angel Hair al Fresco

Angel Hair al Fresco

¾ cup skim milk
1 tablespoon margarine or butter
1 package (4.8 ounces) PASTA RONI™
   Angel Hair Pasta with Herbs
1 can (6⅛ ounces) white tuna in water,
   drained, flaked *or* 1½ cups chopped
   cooked chicken
2 medium tomatoes, chopped
⅓ cup sliced green onions
¼ cup dry white wine or water
¼ cup slivered almonds, toasted
   (optional)
1 tablespoon chopped fresh basil *or*
   1 teaspoon dried basil

1. In 3-quart saucepan, combine 1⅓ cups water, skim milk and margarine. Bring just to a boil.

2. Stir in pasta, contents of seasoning packet, tuna, tomatoes, onions, wine, almonds and basil. Return to a boil; reduce heat to medium.

3. Boil, uncovered, stirring frequently, 6 to 8 minutes. Sauce will be thin, but will thicken upon standing.

4. Let stand 3 minutes or until desired consistency. Stir before serving.

Makes 4 servings

Roasted Vegetables Provençal

8 ounces medium or large mushrooms, halved
1 large zucchini, cut into 1-inch pieces, halved
1 large yellow squash or additional zucchini, cut into 1-inch pieces, quartered
1 large red or green bell pepper, cut into 1-inch pieces
1 small red onion, cut into ¼-inch slices, separated into rings
3 tablespoons olive oil
2 cloves garlic, minced
1 teaspoon dried basil
1 teaspoon dried thyme leaves
½ teaspoon salt (optional)
¼ teaspoon freshly ground black pepper
4 large plum tomatoes, quartered
⅔ cup milk
2 tablespoons margarine or butter
1 package (5.1 ounces) PASTA RONI™ Angel Hair Pasta with Parmesan Cheese

1. Heat oven to 425°F. In 15×10-inch jelly-roll pan combine first 5 vegetables; add combined oil, garlic, basil, thyme, salt and pepper. Toss to coat. Bake 15 minutes; stir in tomatoes. Continue baking 5 to 10 minutes or until vegetables are tender.

2. While vegetables are roasting, combine 1⅓ cups water, milk and margarine in medium saucepan; bring just to a boil. Gradually add pasta while stirring. Stir in contents of seasoning packet. Reduce heat to medium.

3. Boil, uncovered, stirring frequently, 4 minutes. Sauce will be very thin, but will thicken upon standing. Remove from heat.

4. Let stand 3 minutes or until desired consistency. Stir before serving. Serve pasta topped with vegetables.

Makes 4 servings

Stroganoff Noodles & Meatballs

½ pound ground beef or turkey
¼ cup Italian-style dry bread crumbs
1 tablespoon water
1 tablespoon vegetable or olive oil
1½ cups water
½ cup milk
1 package LIPTON® Noodles & Sauce— Stroganoff
1 jar (4.5 ounces) sliced mushrooms, drained
1 teaspoon chopped fresh parsley

In medium bowl, combine ground beef, bread crumbs and 1 tablespoon water. Shape into sixteen 1-inch meatballs. In 10-inch skillet, heat oil and cook meatballs over medium heat 5 minutes or until done; set aside.

In medium saucepan, bring 1½ cups water and milk to a boil. Stir in noodles & sauce— stroganoff and continue boiling over medium heat, stirring occasionally, 7 minutes. Stir in mushrooms, parsley and meatballs and continue cooking, stirring frequently, 3 minutes or until noodles are tender.

Makes 2 (2-cup) servings

Roasted Vegetables Provençal

Flash Primavera

1 pound mostaccioli, ziti or other medium pasta shape, uncooked
1 head broccoli or cauliflower, cut into small florets
1 tablespoon cornstarch
3 cloves garlic, minced
1 (15½-ounce) can low-sodium chicken broth
1 (10-ounce) package frozen mixed vegetables
1 (10-ounce) package frozen chopped spinach, thawed
  Salt and pepper to taste
1 cup grated Parmesan cheese

Prepare pasta according to package directions. Three minutes before pasta is done, stir in broccoli or cauliflower. Drain pasta and vegetables; transfer to large bowl.

In small bowl, dissolve cornstarch in ¼ cup of water. Combine garlic and chicken broth in large saucepan. Simmer over medium heat 3 minutes. Whisk in cornstarch mixture. Stir in mixed vegetables and spinach; cook about 5 minutes or until heated through. Toss sauce and vegetable mixture with pasta. Season with salt and pepper and sprinkle with Parmesan cheese; serve.

Makes 6 servings

*Favorite recipe from **National Pasta Association***

National Pasta Association

The National Pasta Association is the trade association for the U.S. pasta industry. Founded in 1904, the member companies provide a variety of pasta products. Currently, there are about 30 companies producing a record volume of pasta for the insatiable appetites of U.S. consumers.

Pennini with Vegetable Sauce "Springtime"

12 ounces (3 cups) uncooked mostaccioli
1 red bell pepper
2 small zucchini
⅔ cup fresh Oriental pea pods *or* 10 ounces frozen pea pods
3 green onions
4 tablespoons olive oil
2 carrots, cut into julienne strips
1½ cups diced fresh tomatoes
2 tablespoons chopped chives
2 tablespoons fresh chopped dill *or* ½ teaspoon dried dill
  Salt and fresh ground pepper
¼ cup toasted sunflower kernels

Cook pasta according to package directions; drain well. Cut red pepper and zucchini into small slices. Cut pea pods in half or thirds and slice green onions. While pasta is cooking, heat oil in large nonstick saucepan over medium heat. Add red pepper and carrots; cook and stir 6 minutes. Add zucchini, pea pods and onions; cook and stir an additional 5 minutes. Add tomatoes, chives and dill. Season with salt and pepper. Heat until warmed through. Toss vegetable mixture with cooked pasta. Sprinkle with toasted sunflower kernels. Serve hot.

Makes 4 servings

Favorite recipe from **National Sunflower Association**

Zesty Artichoke Basil Sauce

    1 jar (6 ounces) marinated artichoke
        hearts, drained, reserving marinade
    1 cup chopped onions
    1 large clove garlic, minced
    1 can (14½ ounces) CONTADINA®
        Recipe Ready Diced Tomatoes,
        undrained
    1 can (6 ounces) CONTADINA® Tomato
        Paste
    1 cup water
    2 tablespoons chopped fresh basil
    ½ teaspoon salt

In medium saucepan, cook and stir onions and garlic in reserved marinade over medium heat 2 to 3 minutes or until tender. Chop artichoke hearts; add to saucepan with tomatoes, tomato paste, water, basil and salt. Bring to a boil; reduce heat to low. Simmer, uncovered, 20 minutes, stirring occasionally.

Makes 4 cups

Savory Caper and Olive Sauce: Omit artichoke hearts and basil. In medium saucepan, cook and stir onions and garlic in 2 tablespoons olive oil over medium heat 2 to 3 minutes. Add ¾ cup sliced and quartered zucchini, tomatoes, tomato paste, water, salt, 1 can (2¼ ounces) drained sliced pitted ripe olives and 2 tablespoons drained capers. Continue as directed.

Garden Primavera Pasta

    6 ounces bow-tie pasta
    1 jar (6 ounces) marinated artichoke
        hearts
    2 cloves garlic, minced
    ½ teaspoon dried rosemary, crushed
    1 green pepper, cut into thin strips
    1 large carrot, cut into 3-inch julienne
        strips
    1 medium zucchini, cut into 3-inch
        julienne strips
    1 can (14½ ounces) DEL MONTE® Pasta
        Style Chunky Tomatoes
    12 small pitted ripe olives (optional)

Cook pasta according to package directions; drain. Drain artichokes, reserving marinade. Toss pasta in 3 tablespoons artichoke marinade; set aside. Cut artichoke hearts into halves. In large skillet, cook garlic and rosemary in 1 tablespoon artichoke marinade. Add remaining ingredients, except pasta and artichokes. Cook, uncovered, over medium-high heat 4 to 5 minutes or until vegetables are tender-crisp and sauce is thickened. Add artichoke hearts. Spoon over pasta. Serve with grated Parmesan cheese, if desired.

Makes 4 servings

Three Cheese Vegetable Lasagna

1 large onion, chopped
3 cloves garlic, minced
1 teaspoon olive oil
1 can (28 ounces) no-salt-added tomato
  purée
1 can (14½ ounces) no-salt-added
  tomatoes, undrained and chopped
2 cups (6 ounces) sliced fresh
  mushrooms
1 zucchini, diced
1 large green bell pepper, chopped
2 teaspoons basil, crushed
1 teaspoon *each* salt and sugar
  (optional)
½ teaspoon *each* red pepper flakes and
  oregano, crushed
2 cups (15 ounces) SARGENTO® Light
  Ricotta Cheese
1 package (10 ounces) frozen chopped
  spinach, thawed and squeezed dry
2 egg whites
2 tablespoons (½ ounce) SARGENTO®
  Fancy Supreme® Shredded
  Parmesan Cheese
½ pound lasagna noodles, cooked
  according to package directions,
  without oil or salt
¾ cup (3 ounces) *each* SARGENTO®
  Preferred Light® Fancy Shredded
  Mozzarella and Mild Cheddar
  Cheese, divided

Spray large skillet with nonstick vegetable spray. Add onion, garlic and olive oil; cook over medium heat until tender, stirring occasionally. Add tomato purée, tomatoes, tomato liquid, mushrooms, zucchini, bell pepper, basil, salt, sugar, pepper flakes and oregano. Heat to a boil. Reduce heat; cover and simmer 10 minutes or until vegetables are crisp-tender.

Combine Ricotta cheese, spinach, egg whites and Parmesan cheese; mix well. Spread 1 cup sauce in bottom of 13×9-inch baking dish. Layer 3 lasagna noodles over sauce. Top with half of Ricotta cheese mixture and 2 cups of remaining sauce. Repeat layering with 3 more lasagna noodles, remaining Ricotta mixture and 2 cups sauce. Combine Mozzarella and Cheddar cheeses. Sprinkle ¾ cup cheese mixture over sauce. Top with remaining lasagna noodles and sauce. Cover with foil; bake at 375°F 30 minutes. Uncover; bake 15 minutes more. Sprinkle with remaining ¾ cup cheese mixture. Let stand 10 minutes before serving.

Makes 10 servings

Always an industry leader, Sargento was among the first to introduce resealable packaging.

Three Cheese Vegetable Lasagna

Layered Pasta Ricotta Pie

Layered Pasta Ricotta Pie

¼ (1-pound) package CREAMETTE®
   Vermicelli
⅓ cup finely chopped onion
4 cloves garlic, finely chopped
1 tablespoon olive or vegetable oil
1 cup grated fresh Romano cheese
3 eggs
1 (15- or 16-ounce) container ricotta
   cheese
1 (10-ounce) package frozen chopped
   spinach, thawed and well drained
½ teaspoon salt
1 (26-ounce) jar CLASSICO® Di Sicilia
   (Ripe Olives & Mushrooms) Pasta
   Sauce

Preheat oven to 350°F. Break vermicelli
into thirds; cook according to package
directions. Drain. Meanwhile, in large skillet,
cook onion and garlic in oil until tender;
remove from heat. Add cooked vermicelli,
½ cup Romano cheese and *1 egg;* mix well.
Press into well-greased 9-inch springform
pan. Combine *2 egg yolks,* ricotta, spinach,
salt and remaining *½ cup* Romano cheese.
Spread over pasta layer. In small mixer bowl,
beat *2 egg whites* until stiff but not dry; fold
into *1½ cups pasta sauce.* Pour over spinach
mixture. Bake 50 to 60 minutes or until set;
let stand 10 minutes. Heat remaining pasta
sauce; serve with pie. Garnish as desired.
Refrigerate leftovers.

Makes 6 to 8 servings

Lasagna Primavera

1 package (8 ounces) lasagna noodles
3 carrots, cut into ¼-inch slices
1 cup broccoli flowerets
1 cup zucchini, cut into ¼-inch slices
1 crookneck squash, cut into ¼-inch slices
2 (10-ounce) packages frozen chopped spinach, thawed
8 ounces ricotta cheese
1 jar (26 ounces) NEWMAN'S OWN® Marinara Sauce with Mushrooms
12 ounces shredded mozzarella cheese
½ cup grated Parmesan cheese

In 6-quart saucepan, bring 3 quarts water to a boil over high heat. Add lasagna noodles and cook 5 minutes. Add carrots; cook 2 more minutes. Add broccoli, zucchini and crookneck squash; cook 2 minutes more or until pasta is tender. Drain well.

Squeeze liquid out of spinach. Combine spinach with ricotta cheese. In 3-quart rectangular baking pan, spread ⅓ of Newman's Own® Marinara Sauce with Mushrooms. Line pan with lasagna noodles. Place half of vegetables, spinach mixture and mozzarella cheese on noodles. Pour half of remaining sauce over layers. Repeat layers and top with remaining sauce. Sprinkle with Parmesan cheese.

Place baking pan on 15×10-inch baking sheet lined with foil. Bake uncovered in 400°F oven 30 minutes or until hot in center. Let stand 10 minutes before serving. (Casserole may be prepared up to 2 days before baking and refrigerated, covered, until 1 hour before baking. If cold, bake 1 hour at 350°F.) Serve with Italian bread or rolls, green salad with Newman's Own® Light Italian Dressing and red wine.   *Makes 8 servings*

Wild Rice Casserole

¼ pound butter
1 cup uncooked wild rice
½ cup slivered almonds
1 (8-ounce) can mushroom slices, drained
2 tablespoons chives or green onions
3 cups chicken broth

Preheat oven to 325°F. Combine butter, rice, almonds, mushrooms and chives in large saucepan. Cook, stirring constantly, over medium heat to brown rice. Place in medium casserole; add broth. Cover tightly and bake 1 hour.   *Makes 6 servings*

Favorite recipe from **Minnesota Cultivated Wild Rice Council**

Paul Newman's love of Italian food led him to create an enticing line of pasta sauces.
Photo courtesy of Newman's Own, Inc.

The Vegetable Garden

From garden to table, add pizazz to everyday vegetables. Let these delicious recipes be your inspiration for making the ordinary extraordinary.

Grilled Vegetables with Balsamic Vinaigrette

1 medium eggplant (about 1¼ pounds)
2 medium zucchini
2 to 3 medium yellow squash
2 medium red bell peppers
¾ cup olive oil
¼ cup balsamic vinegar
1 teaspoon salt
¼ teaspoon black pepper
1 clove garlic, minced
2 to 3 tablespoons finely chopped
   mixed fresh herbs

Trim, then slice eggplant, zucchini and yellow squash lengthwise into ¼- to ½-inch-thick slices. Core, seed and cut red peppers into 1-inch-wide strips. Place vegetables in deep serving platter or wide shallow casserole. Combine oil, vinegar, salt, pepper, garlic and herbs in small bowl. Pour vinaigrette over vegetables; turn to coat. Let stand 30 minutes or longer. Lift vegetables from vinaigrette, leaving vinaigrette that doesn't cling to vegetables in dish.

Oil hot grid to help prevent sticking. Grill vegetables, on covered grill, over medium KINGSFORD® briquets, 8 to 16 minutes or until fork-tender, turning once or twice. (Time will depend on the vegetable; eggplant takes the longest.) As vegetables are done, return them to platter, then turn to coat with vinaigrette. (Or, cut eggplant, zucchini and yellow squash into cubes, then toss with red peppers and vinaigrette.) Serve warm or at room temperature. *Makes 6 servings*

Grilled Vegetables with Balsamic Vinaigrette

Honey Squash

2 acorn squash (about 6 ounces each)
¼ cup honey
2 tablespoons butter or margarine, melted
2 tablespoons chopped walnuts
2 tablespoons raisins
2 teaspoons Worcestershire sauce

Cut acorn squash lengthwise into halves; do not remove seeds. Place cut side up in baking pan or on baking sheet. Bake at 400°F 30 to 45 minutes or until soft. Remove seeds and fibers.

Combine honey, butter, walnuts, raisins and Worcestershire sauce; spoon into squash. Bake 5 to 10 minutes more or until lightly glazed. *Makes 4 servings*

Favorite recipe from **National Honey Board**

Creamed Spinach à la Lawry's®

4 bacon slices, finely chopped
1 cup finely chopped onions
¼ cup all-purpose flour
2 teaspoons LAWRY'S® Seasoned Salt
½ teaspoon LAWRY'S® Seasoned Pepper
½ teaspoon LAWRY'S® Garlic Powder with Parsley
1½ to 2 cups milk
2 packages (10 ounces each) frozen spinach, cooked and drained

In medium skillet, fry bacon until almost crisp. Add onions to bacon and cook until onions are tender, about 10 minutes. Remove from heat. Add flour, Seasoned Salt, Seasoned Pepper and Garlic Powder with Parsley; blend thoroughly. Gradually add milk, starting with 1½ cups, and stir over low heat until thickened. Add spinach and mix thoroughly. If too thick, add additional milk.

Makes 8 servings

Presentation: Serve with prime ribs of beef.

Spicy Baked Beans

6 bacon slices, cut up
2 cans (1 pound 12 ounces each) baked beans
½ cup firmly packed brown sugar
1 tablespoon bourbon
1 medium onion, chopped
1 tablespoon instant coffee
1 teaspoon dry mustard
¾ teaspoon LAWRY'S® Seasoned Salt
½ to ¾ teaspoon hot pepper sauce
1 can (1 pound 4 ounces) sliced pineapple

In small skillet, brown bacon until soft; drain fat and set aside. In 13×9×2-inch casserole, combine beans, brown sugar, bourbon, onion, coffee, mustard, Seasoned Salt and hot pepper sauce. Let stand at room temperature 30 minutes. Arrange bacon on bean mixture. Layer with pineapple slices. Bake, uncovered, in 375°F oven 40 minutes.

Makes 8 servings

Honey Squash

Roasted Fresh Tomatoes

6 large (about 3 pounds) fresh Florida Tomatoes
2 tablespoons vegetable oil
½ teaspoon basil leaves, crushed
¼ teaspoon thyme leaves, crushed
¼ teaspoon salt
¼ teaspoon ground black pepper

Preheat oven to 425°F. Use tomatoes held at room temperature until fully ripe. Core tomatoes; cut into halves horizontally. Gently squeeze to remove seeds. Place cut side up on rack in broiler pan; set aside. In small bowl, combine oil, basil, thyme, salt and black pepper; brush over cut sides of tomatoes. Place tomatoes cut side down on broiler pan. Bake about 30 minutes or until well browned. Remove tomato skins, if desired. Serve hot, warm or cold.   *Makes 4 to 6 servings*

Favorite recipe from **Florida Tomato Committee**

Lipton® California Mashed Potatoes

2 pounds all-purpose potatoes, peeled, if desired, and cut into chunks
Water
2 tablespoons chopped fresh parsley (optional)
1 envelope LIPTON® RECIPE SECRETS® Onion Soup Mix*
¾ cup milk, heated to boiling
½ cup sour cream

*Also terrific with Lipton® Recipe Secrets® Golden Onion, Golden Herb with Lemon or Savory Herb with Garlic Soup Mix.

In 3-quart saucepan, cover potatoes with water. Bring to a boil over high heat. Reduce heat to low and simmer 20 minutes or until potatoes are very tender; drain. Return potatoes to saucepan. Mash potatoes. Stir in parsley and onion soup mix blended with hot milk and sour cream.

Makes about 6 servings

Classica™ Fontina Potato Surprise

2½ pounds potatoes
3 tablespoons butter or margarine, melted
¼ cup CLASSICA™ Grated Parmesan cheese
1 egg
1 egg white
⅛ teaspoon salt
⅛ teaspoon ground nutmeg
4 tablespoons fine dry bread crumbs, divided
8 ounces CLASSICA™ brand Fontina, cut into chunks
¼ cup freshly grated sharp provolone cheese
¼ pound GALBANI® Prosciutto di Parma, cut into small pieces
2 tablespoons butter or margarine, cut into small pieces

Classica™ Fontina Potato Surprise

In large saucepan, cook potatoes in boiling water over medium-low heat until tender; drain. Cool slightly; peel and cut in half. Press potatoes through food mill or mash until smooth. Combine potatoes, melted butter, Classica™ grated Parmesan cheese, egg, egg white, salt and nutmeg in large bowl; mix until smooth. Set aside.

Sprinkle ½ of bread crumbs in well-buttered 9-inch-round baking dish. Tilt dish to coat.

Spread about ½ of potato mixture on bottom and side of dish.

Combine Classica™ Fontina, provolone and Galbani® Prosciutto di Parma in small bowl. Sprinkle over potato mixture in dish.

Cover with remaining potato mixture; sprinkle with remaining bread crumbs. Dot with pieces of butter.

Bake in preheated 350°F oven 40 minutes or until thin crust forms. Let stand 5 minutes.

Invert baking dish onto serving plate, tapping gently to remove. Serve immediately.

Makes 4 to 6 servings

Easy Glazed Yams

**2 (17- or 23-ounce) cans yams or sweet
    potatoes, drained
¾ cup BAMA® Pineapple or Peach
    Preserves
½ to 1 cup CAMPFIRE® Miniature
    Marshmallows
¼ cup chopped nuts
1 tablespoon margarine or butter**

Preheat oven to 350°F. Arrange yams in
ungreased 1½-quart baking dish. Spoon
preserves over yams; top with marshmallows,
nuts and margarine. Bake 25 minutes or
until hot.   *Makes 4 to 6 servings*

Easy Family Beans

**4 slices bacon
¼ cup chopped onion
2 cans (16 ounces each) HEINZ®
    Vegetarian Beans in Tomato Sauce
    or Pork 'N' Beans
¼ cup HEINZ® Tomato Ketchup
2 to 3 tablespoons light brown sugar
1 teaspoon HEINZ® Worcestershire
    Sauce
Dash garlic powder**

In large skillet, cook bacon until crisp; drain
on paper towels and crumble. Drain fat from
skillet. In same skillet, sauté onion until
tender. Stir in bacon and remaining
ingredients. Simmer, uncovered, about 15
minutes or until desired consistency, stirring
occasionally.
          Makes 6 (about 3½-cup) servings

Photo courtesy of Heinz U.S.A.

Easy Glazed Yams

Fast & Fresh Salads

Get rave reviews from these dazzling salads no matter what the occasion— a main attraction or a perfect accompaniment to any meal.

Hot Taco Salad

¾ pound lean ground beef (80% lean)
½ cup chopped onion
1 package (6.8 ounces) RICE-A-RONI® Beef Flavor
½ cup salsa
1 teaspoon chili powder
4 cups shredded lettuce
1 medium tomato, chopped
½ cup (2 ounces) shredded Monterey Jack or Cheddar cheese
½ cup crushed tortilla chips (optional)

1. In large skillet, brown ground beef and onion; drain. Remove from skillet; set aside.

2. In same skillet, prepare Rice-A-Roni® Mix as package directs.

3. Stir in meat mixture, salsa and chili powder; continue cooking over low heat 3 to 4 minutes or until heated through.

4. Arrange lettuce on serving platter. Top with rice mixture, tomato and cheese. Top with tortilla chips, if desired.

Makes 5 servings

Hot Taco Salad

Golden Gate Chinese Chicken and Cabbage Sesame Salad

1½ pounds boneless, skinless chicken breasts
1½ teaspoons salt-free lemon pepper
¼ teaspoon salt
8 cups thinly sliced napa cabbage
1 medium-size red bell pepper, cut into julienned strips
1 medium-size yellow bell pepper, cut into julienned strips
½ cup diagonally sliced green onions
½ cup sesame seeds, toasted
½ cup chopped dried apricots
3½ teaspoons grated fresh ginger, divided
¼ cup low-sodium chicken broth
¼ cup seasoned rice vinegar
¼ cup low-sodium soy sauce
2 tablespoons sugar
2 tablespoons dark sesame oil
6 napa cabbage leaves
1½ cups chow mein noodles

Place chicken in microproof dish; sprinkle with lemon pepper and salt. Cover with wax paper and microwave on HIGH 8 to 10 minutes or until no longer pink in center, rotating dish half turn every 2 minutes. Or, poach chicken. Remove chicken from dish. Cool; discard liquid. Shred chicken into bite-size pieces. Combine chicken, sliced cabbage, red pepper, yellow pepper, onions, sesame seeds, apricots and 3 teaspoons ginger in large bowl. Toss well; cover and refrigerate until ready to serve. Combine broth, vinegar, soy sauce, sugar, oil and remaining ½ teaspoon ginger in small jar with lid; shake well. Pour over chicken and cabbage mixture; toss gently. Spoon onto individual plates lined with cabbage leaves. Sprinkle evenly with chow mein noodles. Serve immediately. *Makes 6 servings*

Favorite recipe from **National Broiler Council**

Curried Chicken and Chilean Fruit Salad

1 barbecued or roasted chicken, about 2½ pounds, cooled
½ pound green seedless Chilean grapes, halved
2 Chilean Granny Smith apples, peeled, cored and diced
1 extra sweet onion, peeled and chopped
½ cup golden raisins
Juice of ½ lemon
½ cup mayonnaise
½ cup dairy sour cream
1 tablespoon curry powder
Salt and pepper
Leaf lettuce leaves
1 cup slivered almonds, toasted

Cut chicken meat from bones; discard skin. Combine first six ingredients. Whisk mayonnaise, sour cream and curry powder together in small bowl. Pour curried mayonnaise over salad; mix gently. Season to taste with salt and pepper. Line serving platter with lettuce leaves and spoon chicken salad on top. Sprinkle almonds over salad; serve. *Makes 6 to 8 servings*

Favorite recipe from **Chilean Fresh Fruit Association**

Golden Gate Chinese Chicken and Cabbage Sesame Salad

Newman's Own®

For years, Paul Newman packaged homemade salad dressing in old wine bottles for Christmas gifts. One day, he and longtime friend, A. E. Hotchner, decided to market it. The overnight success of Newman's Own Salad Dressing led to expansion of the company's line of all-natural food products to include popcorn, spaghetti sauce, salsa and lemonade. Newman's Own has grown into a multimillion dollar business from which Paul Newman donates 100% of his after-tax profits to charitable and educational causes, including The Hole in the Wall Gang Camp, which he founded in 1988, for children with cancer and other serious blood-related illnesses.

Spinach, Turkey and Apple Salad

¼ cup **NEWMAN'S OWN®** Olive Oil and Vinegar Salad Dressing or **NEWMAN'S OWN®** Light Italian Salad Dressing
4 turkey cutlets, approximately ½ inch thick
4 cups spinach, washed, stems removed
2 Granny Smith apples, cored
¾ cup **NEWMAN'S OWN®** Olive Oil and Vinegar Salad Dressing or **NEWMAN'S OWN®** Light Italian Salad Dressing
⅓ cup crumbled blue cheese
¼ cup walnut halves

Prepare grill or heat broiler.

Brush turkey cutlets with ¼ cup Newman's Own® Salad Dressing; grill turkey cutlets over medium heat or broil as close as possible to heat source, until turkey is no longer pink. Set aside to cool.

Divide spinach among 4 plates. Thinly slice turkey and divide among spinach-lined plates. Thinly slice Granny Smith apples and place on top of turkey. Pour ¾ cup Newman's Own® Salad Dressing evenly over each plate. Top with crumbled blue cheese and walnut halves. *Makes 4 servings*

Party Pasta Salad

Party Pasta Salad

1 package (12 ounces) corkscrew pasta
1 can (20 ounces) DOLE® Pineapple
    Chunks in Juice
1 cup vegetable oil
½ cup distilled white vinegar
1 tablespoon Dijon mustard
1 tablespoon Worcestershire sauce
1 clove garlic, pressed
    Salt and pepper to taste
3 cups DOLE® Cauliflower florettes
3 cups DOLE® Broccoli florettes
1 DOLE® Red Bell Pepper, seeded,
    chunked
1 cup DOLE® Whole Natural Almonds,
    toasted

• Cook noodles according to package directions.

• Drain pineapple; reserve 3 tablespoons juice for dressing.

• For dressing, combine reserved juice, oil, vinegar, mustard, Worcestershire sauce, garlic, salt and pepper in screw-top jar; shake well.

• Combine noodles and cauliflower in large bowl. Pour dressing over salad; toss to coat.

• Cover and marinate in refrigerator overnight.

• Add broccoli, pineapple, red pepper and almonds; toss to coat.

Makes 12 to 15 servings

Albacore Salad Puttanesca with Garlic Vinaigrette

Albacore Salad Puttanesca with Garlic Vinaigrette

2 cups cooked, chilled angel hair pasta
2 cups chopped, peeled plum tomatoes
1 can (4¼ ounces) chopped* ripe
    olives, drained
1 cup Garlic Vinaigrette Dressing
    (recipe follows)
1 can (6 ounces) STARKIST® Solid
    White Tuna, drained and flaked
¼ cup chopped fresh basil leaves

*If you prefer, olives may be sliced rather than chopped.

In large bowl, combine chilled pasta, tomatoes, olives and 1 cup Garlic Vinaigrette Dressing. Add tuna and basil leaves; toss. Serve immediately.   *Makes 2 servings*

Garlic Vinaigrette Dressing

⅓ cup red wine vinegar
2 tablespoons lemon juice
1 to 2 cloves garlic, minced or pressed
1 teaspoon ground black pepper
    Salt to taste
1 cup olive oil

In small bowl, whisk together vinegar, lemon juice, garlic, pepper and salt. Slowly add oil, whisking continuously, until well blended.

Fresh Orange-Pasta Salad

Grated peel of ½ SUNKIST® Orange
Juice of 1 SUNKIST® Orange (⅓ cup)
3 tablespoons olive or vegetable oil
2 teaspoons chopped fresh dill weed *or*
** ½ teaspoon dried dill weed**
¼ teaspoon seasoned salt
2 cups curly or spiral macaroni, cooked
** and drained**
2 SUNKIST® Oranges, peeled and cut
** into half-cartwheel slices**
2 cups broccoli flowerets, cooked and
** drained**
½ cup sliced celery
¼ cup sliced green onions

In large bowl, combine orange peel and juice, oil, dill and seasoned salt. Add remaining ingredients; toss gently. Cover and chill; stir occasionally.   *Makes 6 servings*

Pasta Salad with Pesto and Almonds

1 cup BLUE DIAMOND® Chopped
** Natural Almonds**
1 tablespoon butter
16 ounces corkscrew pasta
1 cup pesto
½ cup freshly grated Parmesan cheese
¼ cup white wine vinegar
¼ cup olive oil
½ teaspoon salt
¼ teaspoon white pepper
1 cup frozen green peas, thawed
4 green onions, sliced
4 ounces cooked ham, julienned
1 red bell pepper, diced

In small skillet, sauté almonds in butter over low heat until crisp; reserve. Cook pasta in salted, boiling water according to manufacturer's directions until just done. Meanwhile, combine pesto, cheese, vinegar, oil, salt and white pepper. When pasta is done, drain and toss hot pasta with peas and pesto dressing. Fold in onions, ham, bell pepper and toasted almonds.
Makes 4 to 6 servings

StarKist's® spokefish and all-time purveyor of good taste.

Southwest Ruffle Salad

⅔ cup **HELLMANN'S®** or **BEST FOODS®**
  Real or Light Mayonnaise or Low
  Fat Mayonnaise Dressing
⅓ **cup sour cream**
¼ **cup chopped cilantro**
2 **tablespoons milk**
2 **tablespoons lime juice**
1 **fresh jalapeño pepper, seeded and**
  minced
1 **teaspoon salt**
7 **ounces MUELLER'S® Pasta Ruffles,**
  cooked, rinsed with cold water and
  drained
2 **large tomatoes, seeded and chopped**
1 **yellow bell pepper, chopped**
1 **zucchini, quartered lengthwise and**
  thinly sliced
3 **green onions, thinly sliced**

In large bowl, combine mayonnaise, sour
cream, cilantro, milk, lime juice, jalapeño
pepper and salt. Add pasta, tomatoes, yellow
bell pepper, zucchini and green onions; toss
to coat well. Garnish as desired. Cover;
refrigerate.   *Makes 6 to 8 servings*

Pasta Twists with Garden Vegetables

8 **ounces uncooked rotelle macaroni**
1 **cup (8 ounces) WISH-BONE® Honey**
  Dijon Dressing
2 **medium tomatoes, finely chopped**
1 **medium green and/or red bell pepper,**
  finely chopped
1 **medium cucumber, sliced**
½ **small red onion, thinly sliced**

Cook macaroni according to package
directions; drain and rinse with cold water
until completely cool.

In large salad bowl, combine honey Dijon
dressing, tomatoes, green pepper, cucumber
and red onion. Toss with macaroni; cover and
chill.   *Makes 8 side-dish servings*

Roasted Tomato and Mozzarella Pasta Salad

3 **cups (8 ounces) rotelle (corkscrew)**
  pasta, uncooked
3 **cups Roasted Fresh Tomatoes**
  (page 82)
1 **cup green bell pepper, cut into ½-inch**
  pieces
¾ **cup (4 ounces) mozzarella cheese,**
  cut into ½-inch pieces
¼ **cup chopped mild red onion**
½ **teaspoon salt**
¼ **teaspoon ground black pepper**
⅓ **cup prepared red wine vinaigrette**
  salad dressing

Cook pasta according to package directions;
rinse and drain. Place in large bowl. Cut
Roasted Fresh Tomatoes in chunks; add to
pasta. Add green pepper, mozzarella cheese,
onion, salt and black pepper. Pour salad
dressing over all; toss to coat. Serve
garnished with basil leaves, if desired.
          Makes 4 servings

Favorite recipe from **Florida Tomato Committee**

Southwest Ruffle Salad

California Table Grape Commission

Table grapes are a very important industry in the state of California which ranks third in worldwide production and supplies 97 percent of the domestically grown table grapes in the U.S. Unlike many fresh fruits, grapes are harvested only when the fruit is ripe. Grapes don't become any sweeter after they are clipped from the vine. Eleven major varieties of grapes are available from May until February, ranging in color from green and red to blue-black. Each has its own unique flavor and texture. The California Table Grape Commission is the promotional arm of the state's fresh grape industry.

Hand-Held Grape Salad with Couscous

1¼ cups chicken broth
1 tablespoon olive oil
1 cup couscous
1½ cups California seedless grapes
1 cup chopped parsley
1 cup peeled, chopped and seeded cucumber
½ cup chopped red or green bell pepper
¼ cup minced green onions
Lemon Mustard Dressing (recipe follows)
8 large green or red lettuce leaves

Combine broth and olive oil in medium saucepan; bring to a boil over high heat. Add couscous. Stir; cover and remove from heat. Let stand 5 minutes. Stir to fluff and cool to room temperature. Add grapes, parsley, cucumber, red pepper, green onions and dressing; mix gently. Place ¼ cup mixture on each lettuce leaf; roll into cone shape and eat out of hand.   *Makes 4 to 6 servings*

Lemon Mustard Dressing: Combine ¼ cup olive oil, 2 tablespoons lemon juice, 2 tablespoons white wine vinegar, 1 clove minced garlic, 1 teaspoon Dijon-style mustard, ½ teaspoon salt and ⅛ teaspoon black pepper; mix well. Makes ½ cup.

Favorite recipe from ***California Table Grape Commission***

Spinach, Bacon and Mushroom Salad

Spinach, Bacon and Mushroom Salad

1 large bunch (12 ounces) fresh
    spinach leaves, washed, drained
    and torn
¾ cup sliced fresh mushrooms
4 slices bacon, cooked and crumbled
¾ cup croutons
4 hard-cooked eggs, finely chopped
    Black pepper, to taste
¾ cup prepared HIDDEN VALLEY
    RANCH® Original Ranch® salad
    dressing

In medium salad bowl, combine spinach,
mushrooms and bacon; toss. Top with
croutons and eggs; season with pepper. Pour
salad dressing over all.   *Makes 6 servings*

Great American Potato Salad

1 cup MIRACLE WHIP® Salad Dressing
1 teaspoon KRAFT® Pure Prepared
  Mustard
½ teaspoon celery seed
½ teaspoon salt
⅛ teaspoon pepper
4 cups cubed cooked potatoes
2 hard-cooked eggs, chopped
½ cup chopped onion
½ cup celery slices
½ cup chopped sweet pickle

Combine salad dressing, mustard, celery seed, salt and pepper; mix well. Add remaining ingredients; mix lightly. Cover; chill.
Makes 6 servings

California Black Bean Salad

1 can (15 ounces) black beans, drained
  and rinsed
1 can (12 ounces) whole kernel corn,
  drained
1 medium tomato, chopped
½ cup chopped red onion
½ cup chopped green bell pepper
½ teaspoon LAWRY'S® Garlic Powder
  with Parsley
  Spicy Mexican Dressing
  (page 100)

In large bowl, combine beans, corn, tomato, onion, bell pepper and Garlic Powder with Parsley; blend well. Toss with dressing; refrigerate 15 minutes.   *Makes 6 servings*

Gloria's Pesto Salad

Dressing
1 cup mayonnaise
2 tablespoons prepared pesto

Salad
4 cups peeled diced potatoes, cooked
½ cup chopped celery
½ cup sliced green onions
½ cup diced red bell pepper
1½ cups (6 ounces) Wisconsin Monterey
  Jack cheese, cubed
1 tablespoon grated Wisconsin
  Parmesan cheese

In small bowl, combine dressing ingredients; set aside. In medium bowl, combine potatoes, celery, onions, pepper and Monterey Jack cheese. Add dressing. Toss lightly. Sprinkle with Parmesan cheese. Chill.
Makes 6 servings

Tip: Wisconsin Style Havarti® cheese delivers the same creamy texture when substituted for Monterey Jack cheese in this recipe.

*Favorite recipe from **Wisconsin Milk Marketing Board***

Great American Potato Salad

Creamy Mexican Dressing con Cilantro

¾ cup dairy sour cream
⅓ cup mayonnaise
⅓ cup buttermilk
3 to 4 tablespoons minced cilantro
1 tablespoon lemon juice
1 tablespoon water
½ teaspoon LAWRY'S® Seasoned Salt
¼ teaspoon basil
¼ teaspoon dry mustard
¼ teaspoon LAWRY'S® Seasoned Pepper
⅛ teaspoon LAWRY'S® Garlic Powder with Parsley
⅛ teaspoon oregano

In medium bowl, combine all ingredients with wire whisk or fork; blend well. Refrigerate several hours to blend flavors.

Makes about 1½ cups

Lemon Pear Zest

1 can (16 ounces) Bartlett pear halves
½ lemon, thinly sliced
3 tablespoons lemon juice
2 teaspoons white vinegar
1 tablespoon chopped parsley

Drain pears; reserve ½ cup liquid. Cut pear halves in thirds lengthwise. Place pears and lemon slices in medium bowl. Combine reserved pear liquid, lemon juice and vinegar; mix well. Bring to a boil. Pour over pears. Cover and refrigerate several hours or overnight. Sprinkle with chopped parsley just before serving and stir gently.

Makes 6 servings

Tip: Serve with grilled meat or whitefish.

*Favorite recipe from **Pacific Coast Canned Pear Service***

Citrus Vinaigrette

¼ cup KARO® Light Corn Syrup
¼ cup orange juice
¼ cup cider vinegar
¼ teaspoon grated lime peel
2 tablespoons lime juice
1 tablespoon Dijon mustard
½ teaspoon ground cumin
½ teaspoon salt
½ cup MAZOLA® Corn Oil

In medium bowl, combine corn syrup, orange juice, vinegar, lime peel, lime juice, mustard, cumin and salt. With wire whisk or fork, gradually blend in corn oil. Cover and refrigerate several hours or overnight. Toss with salad greens or serve over sliced avocado or fruit. *Makes about 1⅓ cups*

Basic Olive Oil Vinaigrette

⅓ cup wine or cider vinegar
¼ teaspoon salt
¼ teaspoon black pepper
1 cup FILIPPO BERIO® Extra Virgin Olive Oil

Whisk together vinegar, salt and pepper in small bowl. Slowly whisk in oil until well blended. Serve with salad greens.

Makes 10 servings

Spicy Mexican Dressing

¾ cup Italian-style salad dressing
2 teaspoons chopped cilantro
½ to ¾ teaspoon hot pepper sauce
½ teaspoon LAWRY'S® Seasoned Pepper
½ teaspoon chili powder

In medium bowl, combine all ingredients; blend well. *Makes 3 cups*

Basic Olive Oil Vinaigrette

• **Herb Vinaigrette:** Prepare as directed. Stir in 1 teaspoon *each* dried mustard, basil and tarragon leaves.

• **Balsamic Vinaigrette:** Prepare as directed substituting balsamic vinegar for the wine vinegar. Stir in 1 tablespoon of minced shallots and ¼ teaspoon dried marjoram leaves.

• **Chive Vinaigrette:** Prepare as directed. Stir in 2 teaspoons minced fresh chives.

• **Creamy Dijon Vinaigrette:** Prepare as directed; whisk in 2 teaspoons Dijon mustard and ½ tablespoon mayonnaise.

• **Honey-Dijon Vinaigrette:** Prepare as directed; whisk in 1 tablespoon Dijon mustard and 2 tablespoons honey.

• **Mint Vinaigrette:** Prepare as directed. Stir in 2 tablespoons chopped fresh mint.

• **Parmesan Vinaigrette:** Prepare as directed. Stir in 1 tablespoon Parmesan cheese.

Best Brunches & Lunches

Celebrate all occasions with an impressive array of taste sensations. These irrestible recipes are perfect for a bountiful late-morning brunch or leisurely midday lunch.

Western Omelet

½ cup finely chopped red or green bell pepper
½ cup cubed cooked potato
2 slices turkey bacon, diced
¼ teaspoon dried oregano leaves
2 teaspoons FLEISCHMANN'S® Margarine, divided
1 cup EGG BEATERS® Real Egg Product
Fresh oregano sprig, for garnish

In 8-inch skillet, over medium heat, sauté bell pepper, potato, turkey bacon and dried oregano in 1 teaspoon margarine until tender.* Remove from skillet; keep warm.

In same skillet, over medium heat, melt remaining 1 teaspoon margarine. Pour Egg Beaters® into skillet. Cook, lifting edges to allow uncooked portion to flow underneath. When almost set, spoon vegetable mixture over half of omelet. Fold other half over vegetable mixture; slide onto serving plate. Garnish with fresh oregano.

Makes 2 servings

*For frittata, sauté vegetables and turkey bacon in 2 teaspoons margarine. Pour Egg Beaters® evenly into skillet over prepared vegetables. Cook without stirring for 4 to 5 minutes or until cooked on bottom and almost set on top. Carefully turn frittata; cook for 1 to 2 minutes more or until done. Slide onto serving platter; cut into wedges to serve.

Western Omelet

Country Fare Breakfast with Wisconsin Fontina

¼ cup butter
2 cups frozen hash brown potatoes
¼ cup finely chopped onion
6 eggs, beaten
¾ teaspoon salt
⅛ teaspoon pepper
2 tablespoons milk
¼ cup chopped parsley, divided
1 cup (4 ounces) shredded Wisconsin Fontina cheese, divided
1 cup cubed cooked turkey

Melt butter in 10-inch ovenproof skillet; add potatoes and onion. Cook, covered, over medium heat 15 minutes until tender and lightly browned; stir occasionally. Beat together eggs, salt, pepper and milk; stir in 3 tablespoons parsley and ½ cup cheese. Pour egg mixture over potatoes; sprinkle with turkey. Bake, uncovered, in preheated 350°F oven for 20 minutes or until eggs are set. Sprinkle remaining ½ cup cheese over eggs; return to oven for about 2 minutes until cheese is melted. Remove from oven and garnish with remaining 1 tablespoon parsley. Cut into wedges and serve with salsa, if desired. *Makes 6 servings*

Note: Ham may be substituted for turkey.

Favorite recipe from **Wisconsin Milk Marketing Board**

Hearty Breakfast Custard Casserole

1 pound (2 medium-large) Colorado baking potatoes
Salt and pepper
8 ounces bulk low-fat sausage, cooked and crumbled, *or* 6 ounces finely diced lean ham *or* 6 ounces turkey bacon, cooked and crumbled
⅓ cup julienne-sliced roasted red pepper *or* 2-ounce jar sliced pimentos
3 eggs
1 cup low-fat milk
3 tablespoons chopped chives or green onion tops, *or* ¾ teaspoon dried thyme or oregano leaves
Salsa and low-fat yogurt (optional)

Heat oven to 375°F. Butter 8- or 9-inch square baking dish or other small casserole. Peel potatoes and slice very thin; arrange half of potatoes in prepared baking dish. Sprinkle with salt and pepper. Cover with half of sausage or ham. Arrange remaining potatoes on top; sprinkle with salt and pepper. Top with remaining sausage and red pepper. Beat eggs, milk and chives until blended. Pour over potatoes. Cover baking dish with aluminum foil and bake 35 to 45 minutes, or until potatoes are tender. Uncover and bake 5 to 10 minutes more. Serve with salsa and yogurt, if desired. *Makes 4 to 5 servings*

Favorite recipe from **Colorado Potato Administrative Committee**

Country Fare Breakfast with Wisconsin Fontina

Cheese-Bacon Soufflé

Grated Parmesan cheese
2 tablespoons butter
¼ cup chopped green onions
2 tablespoons all-purpose flour
¼ teaspoon salt
⅛ teaspoon pepper
⅛ teaspoon garlic powder
1 cup milk
1 cup (4 ounces) shredded Cheddar cheese
3 egg yolks, slightly beaten
3 egg whites
¼ teaspoon cream of tartar
6 slices bacon, cooked, drained and crumbled

Preheat oven to 350°F. Butter 1½-quart soufflé dish or casserole. Sprinkle enough Parmesan cheese in dish to coat bottom and side evenly; remove any excess. Melt butter in medium-sized saucepan. Sauté green onions until tender, about 3 minutes. Blend in flour, salt, pepper and garlic powder. Remove from heat; stir in milk. Heat to boiling, stirring constantly. Boil and stir 1 minute. Remove from heat and stir in Cheddar cheese until melted. If necessary, return to low heat to finish melting cheese. *(Do not boil.)* Blend a little of hot mixture into egg yolks; return all to saucepan. Blend thoroughly; set aside. Beat egg whites until frothy. Add cream of tartar and beat until soft peaks form. Fold cheese sauce into egg whites. Fold in bacon. Turn into prepared soufflé dish. Bake 40 to 45 minutes. Serve immediately.

Makes 2 servings

*Favorite recipe from **American Dairy Association***

Crowd-Sized Spinach Soufflé

Butter
Grated Parmesan cheese
2 cups milk
½ cup quick-cooking tapioca
4 teaspoons instant minced onion
1 tablespoon instant chicken bouillon
⅛ teaspoon ground nutmeg
1 cup (4 ounces) shredded Swiss cheese
8 eggs, separated
1 teaspoon cream of tartar
2 packages (10 ounces each) frozen chopped spinach, thawed and well drained

Butter bottom and sides of 13×9×2-inch baking dish. Dust with Parmesan cheese. Set aside.

In medium saucepan, stir together milk, tapioca, onion, bouillon and nutmeg. Let stand 10 minutes. Cook over medium-high heat, stirring constantly, until mixture boils and is thickened. Stir in Swiss cheese until melted. Set aside.

In large bowl, beat egg whites with cream of tartar at high speed until stiff but not dry, just until whites no longer slip when bowl is tilted. Thoroughly blend egg yolks and spinach into reserved sauce. Gently, but thoroughly, fold yolk mixture into whites. Carefully pour into prepared dish. Bake in preheated 350°F oven 30 to 40 minutes or until puffy, delicately browned and soufflé shakes slightly when oven rack is gently moved back and forth. Serve immediately.

Makes 8 servings

*Favorite recipe from **American Egg Board***

Crab & Shrimp Quiche

Crab & Shrimp Quiche

6 slices BORDEN® Process American
    Cheese Food
2 tablespoons sliced green onion
2 tablespoons chopped pimiento
1 tablespoon all-purpose flour
1 (6-ounce) can ORLEANS® or HARRIS®
    Crab Meat, drained
1 (4¼-ounce) can ORLEANS® Shrimp,
    drained and soaked as label directs
1½ cups BORDEN® or MEADOW GOLD®
    Half-and-Half
3 eggs, beaten
1 (9-inch) unbaked pastry shell

Place rack in lowest position in oven; preheat oven to 425°F. Cut *4 slices* cheese food into pieces. In large bowl, toss cheese food pieces, onion and pimiento with flour. Add crab meat, shrimp, half-and-half and eggs. Pour into pastry shell. Bake 20 minutes. Reduce oven temperature to 325°F; bake 20 minutes longer or until set. Arrange remaining *2 slices* cheese food on top of quiche. Let stand 10 minutes before serving. Garnish as desired. Refrigerate leftovers.

Makes one 9-inch quiche

America's Favorite Cheddar Beef Burgers

1 pound ground beef
⅓ cup A.1.® Steak Sauce
1 medium onion, cut into strips
1 medium green or red bell pepper, cut into strips
1 tablespoon margarine
4 ounces Cheddar cheese, sliced
4 hamburger rolls
4 tomato slices

In medium bowl, combine ground beef and 3 tablespoons steak sauce; shape mixture into 4 patties. Set aside.

In medium skillet, over medium heat, cook onion and pepper in margarine until tender, stirring occasionally. Stir in remaining steak sauce; keep warm.

Grill burgers over medium heat 4 minutes on each side or until done. When almost done, top with cheese; grill until cheese melts. Spoon 2 tablespoons onion mixture onto each roll bottom; top each with burger, tomato slice, some of remaining onion mixture and roll top. *Makes 4 servings*

Lipton® Onion Burgers

1 envelope LIPTON® RECIPE SECRETS® Onion Soup Mix*
2 pounds ground beef
½ cup water

*Also terrific with Lipton® Recipe Secrets® Beefy Onion, Onion-Mushroom or Italian Herb with Tomato Soup Mix.

In large bowl, combine soup mix, beef and water; shape into 8 patties. Grill or broil until done. *Makes about 8 servings*

Suggestion: Serve with lettuce, tomato, pickles and potato salad.

Wisconsin Cheese Burgers

3 pounds ground beef
½ cup dry bread crumbs
2 eggs, beaten
1¼ cups (5 ounces) of your favorite shredded Wisconsin cheese, Pepper Havarti cheese, shredded, Blue cheese, crumbled, or Basil & Tomato Feta cheese, crumbled

In large bowl, combine beef, bread crumbs and eggs; mix well, but lightly. Divide mixture into 24 balls; flatten each on waxed paper to 4 inches across. Place 1 heaping tablespoonful cheese on each of 12 patties. Top with remaining patties, carefully pressing edges to seal. Grill patties 4 inches from coals, turning only once, 6 to 9 minutes on each side or until no longer pink. To keep cheese between patties as it melts, do not flatten burgers with spatula while grilling. *Makes 12 servings*

Caution: Cheese filling may be very hot if eaten immediately after cooking.

*Favorite recipe from **Wisconsin Milk Marketing Board***

America's Favorite Cheddar Beef Burger

Philadelphia Cheese Steak Sandwiches

2 cups sliced red or green bell peppers (about 2 medium)
1 small onion, thinly sliced
1 tablespoon vegetable oil
½ cup A.1.® BOLD Steak Sauce
1 teaspoon prepared horseradish
8 ounces thinly sliced beef sandwich steaks
4 long sandwich rolls, split
4 ounces thinly sliced mozzarella cheese

In medium saucepan, over medium heat, sauté bell peppers and onion in oil until tender. Stir in steak sauce and horseradish; keep warm.

In lightly greased medium skillet, over medium-high heat, cook sandwich steaks until done. On roll bottoms, portion beef, pepper mixture and cheese.

Broil sandwich bottoms 4 inches from heat source 3 to 5 minutes or until cheese melts; replace tops. Serve immediately.

Makes 4 sandwiches

Chicken Po' Boy Sandwich

½ cup fat free, cholesterol free mayonnaise
1 tablespoon Dijon mustard
2 teaspoons cider vinegar
½ teaspoon dried thyme
¼ teaspoon ground red pepper
3½ tablespoons all-purpose flour
2 green onions, minced
1 teaspoon paprika
1 pound COOKIN' GOOD® Tenderloins of Chicken Breast, thawed
2 tablespoons vegetable oil, divided
1 long loaf Italian or French bread
½ head red leaf lettuce
1 large tomato, sliced

1. In small bowl, combine mayonnaise, mustard, vinegar, thyme and ground red pepper; set aside.

2. In plastic bag or on wax paper, combine flour, green onions and paprika. Add chicken, a few pieces at a time, tossing to coat with flour mixture. Repeat with remaining chicken pieces.

3. In 10-inch skillet over medium heat, heat 1 tablespoon vegetable oil. Cook half of chicken pieces 3 to 4 minutes or until no longer pink, turning once. Repeat with remaining 1 tablespoon oil and chicken pieces.

4. To serve, cut bread in half horizontally. Place lettuce leaves on bottom half of bread. Arrange chicken pieces and tomato slices on top of lettuce. Spread mayonnaise mixture on top half of bread. Replace top of bread. Cut bread crosswise into 4 pieces.

Makes 4 servings

Philadelphia Cheese Steak Sandwich

Soft Shell Chicken Tacos

¾ **pound boneless, skinless chicken**
    breasts
1 **teaspoon ground cumin**
1 **can (8 ounces) stewed tomatoes**
⅓ **cup salsa**
1 **green onion, thinly sliced**
8 **(7-inch) flour tortillas, warmed**
1 **cup shredded lettuce**
1 **medium tomato, chopped**
1 **cup (4 ounces) SARGENTO®**
    Preferred Light® Shredded Cheese
    For Tacos
¼ **cup chopped fresh cilantro (optional)**

Place chicken in single layer in skillet; season with cumin. Pour tomatoes and salsa over chicken. Simmer, uncovered, 15 minutes or until chicken is tender, turning once. Remove chicken; save liquid in skillet. Cool and shred chicken; add to skillet with green onion. Cook 2 minutes or until most of the liquid is absorbed. Divide chicken mixture evenly down center of each tortilla. Top with shredded lettuce, chopped fresh tomato and taco cheese. Add cilantro; fold and serve immediately. *Makes 4 servings*

Sargento

It was in Plymouth, in the heart of Wisconsin's dairyland, that Leonard Gentine, Sr. launched the Plymouth Cheese Counter in the late 1940s. Gentine noticed there was a great demand for smaller-sized packaged cheese products versus the larger bulk sizes sold in retail stores. To satisfy this demand, Gentine went into partnership with Joseph Sartori and formed the Sargento Cheese Company in 1953. Consumer-sized packages of Mozzarella, Provolone and Romano were the company's first products. As consumers expressed more interest in convenience products, Sargento was the first company to introduce shredded and sliced natural cheeses, and the first zippered resealable packaging for perishable food products.

Tuna Melt

Tuna Melt

1 can (12 ounces) STARKIST® Solid
   White or Chunk Light Tuna, drained
   and flaked
⅓ cup mayonnaise
1½ tablespoons sweet pickle relish
1½ tablespoons chopped onion
½ tablespoon mustard
3 English muffins, split and toasted
6 tomato slices, halved
6 slices American, Cheddar, Swiss or
   Monterey Jack cheese
   Fresh fruit (optional)

In medium bowl, combine tuna, mayonnaise, pickle relish, onion and mustard; mix well. Spread about ⅓ cup on each muffin half. Top with tomato slice and cheese slice. Broil 4 to 5 minutes or until cheese melts. Serve with fresh fruit, if desired.   *Makes 6 servings*

The Bountiful Bread Basket

Fill your kitchen with the enticing aroma of home-baked breads. This oven-loving collection of heartwarming recipes is abounding with homemade goodness.

Mott's® Morning Glory Bread

2½ cups all-purpose flour
2 teaspoons baking powder
1 teaspoon baking soda
½ teaspoon salt
½ teaspoon cinnamon
¼ teaspoon nutmeg
¼ teaspoon allspice
¾ cup granulated sugar
¾ cup light brown sugar
1 tablespoon GRANDMA'S® Molasses
3 egg whites
½ cup MOTT'S® Chunky Apple Sauce
1 tablespoon vegetable oil
¾ cup grated carrots
½ cup raisins
⅓ cup crushed pineapple, drained
¼ cup shredded coconut

1. Preheat oven to 375°F. Spray 8½×4½×3-inch loaf pan with nonstick cooking spray.

2. In medium bowl, combine flour, baking powder, baking soda, salt and spices.

3. In separate large bowl, mix together sugars, molasses, egg whites, apple sauce and vegetable oil.

4. Add flour mixture to apple sauce mixture and stir until mixture is combined. Fold in carrots, raisins, pineapple and coconut.

5. Pour batter into prepared pan and bake 45 to 50 minutes or until toothpick inserted in center comes out clean.

Makes 18 servings

From left to right: Mott's® Lemon Poppy Seed Tea Loaf (page 116) and Mott's® Morning Glory Bread

Mott's® Lemon Poppy Seed Tea Loaf

2 tablespoons vegetable oil
⅔ cup MOTT'S® Natural Apple Sauce
1 cup granulated sugar
1 whole egg
2 egg whites, slightly beaten
1 teaspoon vanilla
2½ cups all-purpose flour
2 teaspoons baking powder
½ teaspoon baking soda
½ teaspoon salt
¼ cup poppy seed
1 tablespoon grated lemon peel
⅓ cup skim milk

Lemon Syrup
¼ cup lemon juice
¼ cup granulated sugar

1. Preheat oven to 350°F. Spray 9×5×4-inch loaf pan with nonstick cooking spray.

2. In large bowl, combine oil, Mott's® Natural Apple Sauce, 1 cup granulated sugar, egg, beaten egg whites and vanilla.

3. In separate medium bowl, combine flour, baking powder, baking soda, salt, poppy seed and lemon peel.

4. Add flour mixture to apple sauce mixture alternately with skim milk. Mix until ingredients are thoroughly moistened.

5. Pour batter into prepared pan. Bake 30 to 35 minutes or until toothpick inserted in center comes out clean. Cool loaf in pan on cooling rack.

6. Heat lemon juice and ¼ cup granulated sugar in small saucepan until sugar dissolves. Remove from heat and cool.

7. Remove cake from pan and return to cooling rack. Pierce loaf all over with metal skewer. Brush loaf with prepared lemon syrup. Let stand until cool. Slice thinly to serve. *Makes 20 servings*

Mott's was founded in 1842 when Sam R. Mott began making cider and vinegar in a small mill in Bouckville, New York. These products caught the fancy of his neighbors and as demand grew so did the size of his mill. In 1900, Mott merged with the W.B. Duffy Cider Company. Sam Mott quickly incorporated Duffy's method for preserving apple cider in wood which further increased the size of the market. In 1930, apple sauce was added to the Mott's line. Today, Mott's produces over 13 million cases of apple juice and apple sauce every year.

Colorful Veg-All® Cornbread

Colorful Veg-All®
Cornbread

1 (8½-ounce) box cornbread mix
1 (16-ounce) can VEG-ALL® Mixed
   Vegetables, drained
1 cup shredded Cheddar cheese
½ cup chopped onion
⅓ cup milk
1 egg, slightly beaten

Combine cornbread mix, vegetables, cheese, onion, milk and egg. (Leftover chopped, cooked ham or sausage can be added.) Spoon into lightly greased 8×8-inch pan. Bake in preheated 400°F oven 25 minutes. Cool 5 minutes before cutting.

Makes 6 to 8 servings

Generations of Americans have depended on Libby's Solid Pack Pumpkin for the very best holiday pumpkin pies—in fact, for many people, a slice of Libby's Famous Pumpkin Pie is the only way to finish the eagerly awaited holiday meal. Libby began its pumpkin processing operations in 1929 after years of research to develop their own strain of pumpkin that is meaty, sweet and less watery than pumpkins found at the local market. Minimal processing during canning yields a 100% pure product that is always high quality.

Pumpkin Pecan Bread

1 cup butter, softened
1 cup granulated sugar
1 cup packed dark brown sugar
4 eggs
1 cup LIBBY'S® Solid Pack Pumpkin
2¾ cups all-purpose flour
1 tablespoon pumpkin pie spice
2 teaspoons baking powder
1 teaspoon baking soda
½ teaspoon salt
1 cup pecans, finely chopped

CREAM butter, granulated sugar and brown sugar in large mixer bowl until light. Add eggs, one at a time, beating well after each addition. Beat in pumpkin.

COMBINE flour, pumpkin pie spice, baking powder, baking soda, salt and pecans in small bowl. Add to pumpkin mixture; mix just until blended.

SPOON into 2 greased and floured 8½×4½-inch loaf pans.

BAKE in preheated 350°F oven for 1 hour 10 minutes, or until wooden pick inserted in center comes out clean. Cool for 10 minutes. Remove from pans; cool on wire racks.

Makes 2 loaves

Cherry Oatmeal Muffins

1 cup individually quick frozen tart cherries
1⅛ cups quick-cooking oats, uncooked
1 cup buttermilk
1 egg, beaten
¾ cup firmly packed brown sugar
½ cup solid vegetable shortening, melted and cooled
1 cup all-purpose flour
1½ teaspoons baking powder
½ teaspoon salt

Cut cherries in half; set aside. In large bowl, combine oats and buttermilk; mix well. Let stand 1 hour.

In another large bowl, combine egg, brown sugar and shortening. Add egg mixture to oats mixture. Mix with electric mixer on low speed 30 seconds; scrape side of bowl.

Cherry Oatmeal Muffiins

In small bowl, combine flour, baking powder and salt. Add flour mixture to oats mixture; mix until ingredients are moistened. Fold in cherries with spoon or rubber spatula.

Fill 12 greased muffin cups two-thirds full. Bake in preheated 400°F oven 15 to 20 minutes.   *Makes 12 muffins*

Note: 1 cup canned tart cherries, well drained and halved, or 1 cup chopped dried cherries may be substituted for 1 cup individually quick frozen tart cherries.

Favorite recipe from **Cherry Marketing Institute, Inc.**

Biscuits

2 cups sifted all-purpose flour
3 teaspoons baking powder
1 teaspoon salt
⅓ CRISCO® Stick or ⅓ cup CRISCO®
    all-vegetable shortening
¾ cup milk

1. **Heat** oven to 425°F. **Combine** flour, baking powder and salt in bowl. **Cut** in shortening using pastry blender (or 2 knives) until mixture resembles coarse meal. **Add** milk; **stir** with fork until blended.

2. **Transfer** dough to lightly floured surface. **Knead** gently 8 to 10 times. **Roll** dough ½ inch thick. **Cut** with floured 2-inch-round cutter.

3. **Bake** on ungreased cookie sheet for 12 to 15 minutes.

Makes 12 to 16 (2-inch) biscuits

The Original Kellogg's® All-Bran Muffin™

1¼ cups all-purpose flour
½ cup sugar
1 tablespoon baking powder
¼ teaspoon salt
2 cups KELLOGG'S® ALL-BRAN® Cereal
1¼ cups milk
1 egg
¼ cup vegetable oil
    Vegetable cooking spray

1. Stir together flour, sugar, baking powder and salt. Set aside.

2. In large mixing bowl, combine Kellogg's® All-Bran® cereal and milk. Let stand about 5 minutes or until cereal softens. Add egg and oil. Beat well. Add flour mixture, stirring only until combined. Portion batter evenly into twelve 2½-inch muffin-pan cups coated with cooking spray.

3. Bake at 400°F about 20 minutes or until lightly browned. Serve warm.

Makes 12 muffins

Crisco® was packaged in glass jars during World War II because of metal shortages.

Cherry Cheese Muffins

1 package (17¼ ounces) frozen puff pastry, thawed
2½ cups Northwest sweet cherries, pitted and halved
½ cup sugar
1 tablespoon cornstarch
1 teaspoon grated orange peel
Cheese Filling (recipe follows)
Egg Glaze (recipe follows)

Roll each pastry sheet into 15×10-inch rectangle. Cut each sheet into 6 (5×5-inch) squares. Arrange in muffin pans. Combine cherries, sugar, cornstarch and orange peel; mix thoroughly. Fill pastry with 3 to 4 tablespoons Cheese Filling; divide cherry mixture evenly and spoon over filling. Pull corners of pastry to center and pinch to partially seal. Brush with Egg Glaze. Bake in preheated 400°F oven 20 to 25 minutes or until pastry has puffed and cherry filling is thick and bubbly. *Makes 12 muffins*

Cheese Filling: Beat 1 package (8 ounces) cream cheese, softened, ¼ cup sugar, 1 egg and 2 tablespoons orange juice until smooth. Makes about 1¾ cups.

Egg Glaze: Combine 1 egg, beaten, and 1 tablespoon water; mix thoroughly.

Favorite recipe from **Northwest Cherry Growers**

Apple 'n Walnut Spiced Muffins

1 cup raisins
2 cups all-purpose flour
1 cup oatmeal
⅔ cup sugar
2½ teaspoons baking powder
½ teaspoon salt
½ teaspoon ground cinnamon
½ teaspoon ground allspice
¼ teaspoon ground nutmeg
4 to 5 small apples
1 egg
2 egg whites
¼ cup canola oil or vegetable oil
½ cup chopped California walnuts

Preheat oven to 350°F. Grease muffin tins or spray with nonstick cooking spray.

Pour hot water over raisins in small bowl and let sit 10 minutes; drain well and set aside.

Meanwhile, in medium bowl, combine flour, oatmeal, sugar, baking powder, salt, cinnamon, allspice and nutmeg. Stir and toss to combine; set aside.

Peel and core apples. Grate coarsely—you need about 2 generous cups, lightly pressed down. Combine grated apples, egg, egg whites, oil and walnuts; beat to blend. Add to combined dry ingredients and raisins; stir just until blended and moistened—batter will be very stiff. Spoon into prepared muffin tins, filling about three-quarters full. Bake 20 to 25 minutes, or until wooden pick inserted in muffin comes out clean. Cool 5 minutes in pan; remove and serve warm. *Makes 12 muffins*

Favorite recipe from **Walnut Marketing Board**

Good Old American White Rolls

5 to 5½ cups all-purpose flour
2 packages RED STAR® Active Dry
   Yeast or QUICK•RISE™ Yeast
2 tablespoons sugar
4 tablespoons nonfat dry milk
2 teaspoons salt
1½ cups water
1 tablespoon shortening or oil
3 tablespoons melted butter
2 teaspoons honey

Preheat oven to 400°F. In large mixer bowl, combine 2½ cups flour, yeast, sugar, milk and salt; mix well. In saucepan, heat water and shortening until very warm (120°–130°F; shortening does not need to melt). Add to flour mixture. Blend at low speed until moistened; beat 3 minutes at medium speed. By hand, gradually stir in enough remaining flour to make firm dough. Knead on floured surface until smooth and elastic 5 to 8 minutes. Place in greased bowl, turning to grease top. Cover; let rise in warm place until doubled, about 45 minutes (30 minutes for Quick•Rise™ Yeast).

Punch down dough. Divide dough into 2 parts. Divide each part into 6 to 12 equal pieces (depending on what size, 1 ounce or 2 ounces, finished product is desired). Round into smooth balls. Place on greased cookie sheet. Cover; let rise in warm place until about doubled, 25 to 30 minutes (15 to 20 minutes for Quick•Rise™ Yeast). Bake at 400°F for 10 to 12 minutes until golden brown. Mix melted butter and honey together; brush rolls with honey-butter mixture. Remove from cookie sheet and cool.

Makes 12 to 24 rolls

Pecan Sticky Buns

Dough*

4½ to 5½ cups all-purpose flour, divided
½ cup granulated sugar
1½ teaspoons salt
2 packages active dry yeast
¾ cup warm milk (105° to 115°F)
½ cup warm water (105° to 115°F)
¼ cup (½ stick) MAZOLA® Margarine or
   butter, softened
2 eggs

Glaze

½ cup KARO® Light or Dark Corn Syrup
½ cup packed light brown sugar
¼ cup (½ stick) MAZOLA® Margarine or
   butter
1 cup pecans, coarsely chopped

Filling

½ cup firmly packed light brown sugar
1 teaspoon cinnamon
2 tablespoons MAZOLA® Margarine or
   butter, melted

***To use frozen bread dough:** Thaw two 1-pound loaves frozen bread dough in refrigerator overnight. Press loaves together and roll to 20×12-inch rectangle; complete as recipe directs.

For Dough: In large bowl combine 2 cups flour, sugar, salt and yeast. Stir in milk, water and ¼ cup margarine until blended. Stir in eggs and enough additional flour (about 2 cups) to make a soft dough. Knead on floured surface until smooth and elastic, about 8 minutes. Cover dough and let rest on floured surface 10 minutes.

Pecan Sticky Buns

For Glaze: Meanwhile, in small saucepan over low heat stir corn syrup, ½ cup brown sugar and ¼ cup margarine until smooth. Pour into 13×9×2-inch baking pan. Sprinkle with pecans; set aside.

For Filling: Combine ½ cup brown sugar and cinnamon; set aside. Roll dough to 20×12-inch rectangle. Brush dough with 2 tablespoons melted margarine; sprinkle with filling. Starting from long side, roll up jelly-roll fashion. Pinch seam to seal. Cut into 15 slices. Place cut side up in prepared pan. Cover tightly. Refrigerate 2 to 24 hours.

To bake, preheat oven to 375°F. Remove pan from refrigerator. Uncover pan and let stand at room temperature 10 minutes. Bake 28 to 30 minutes or until tops are browned. Invert onto serving tray. Serve warm or cool completely.   *Makes 15 rolls*

For Chocolate Lovers Only

Rediscover the world of delectable chocolate. From decadent cakes and pies to sumptuous brownies and fudge, these sinful pleasures will surely satisfy any die-hard chocoholic.

Wellesley Fudge Cake

4 squares BAKER'S® Unsweetened Chocolate
1¾ cups sugar, divided
½ cup water
1⅔ cups flour
1 teaspoon baking soda
¼ teaspoon salt
½ cup (1 stick) butter or margarine, softened
3 eggs
¾ cup milk
1 teaspoon vanilla

HEAT oven to 350°F.

MICROWAVE chocolate, ½ cup sugar and water in large microwavable bowl on HIGH 1 to 2 minutes or until chocolate is almost melted, stirring halfway through heating time. Stir until chocolate is completely melted; cool.

MIX flour, baking soda and salt; set aside. Beat butter and remaining 1¼ cups sugar in large bowl with electric mixer on medium speed until light and fluffy. Add eggs, 1 at a time, beating well after each addition. Add flour mixture alternately with milk, beating after each addition until smooth. Stir in chocolate mixture and vanilla. Pour into 2 greased and floured 9-inch round cake pans.

BAKE 30 to 35 minutes or until cake springs back when lightly touched. Cool 10 minutes; remove from pans. Cool on wire racks. Frost as desired. *Makes 12 servings*

From top to bottom: German Sweet Chocolate Cake (page 126) and Wellesley Fudge Cake

Baker's Chocolate

In 1765, an Irish immigrant named John Hannon received financial help from Dr. James Baker when he started milling chocolate in Dorchester, Massachusetts. In 1852, a new kind of chocolate was introduced, Baker's German's sweet chocolate, named for Samuel German, who helped perfect this delectable sweet chocolate.

German Sweet Chocolate Cake

1 package (4 ounces) BAKER'S®
   GERMAN'S® Sweet Chocolate
½ cup water
2 cups all-purpose flour
1 teaspoon baking soda
¼ teaspoon salt
1 cup (2 sticks) butter or margarine,
   softened
2 cups sugar
4 egg yolks
1 teaspoon vanilla
1 cup buttermilk
4 egg whites
   Classic Coconut-Pecan Filling and
   Frosting (page 128)

HEAT oven to 350°F. Line bottoms of 3 (9-inch) round cake pans with waxed paper.

MICROWAVE chocolate and water in large microwavable bowl on HIGH 1½ to 2 minutes or until chocolate is almost melted, stirring halfway through heating time. *Stir until chocolate is completely melted.*

MIX flour, baking soda and salt; set aside. Beat butter and sugar in large bowl with electric mixer on medium speed until light and fluffy. Add egg yolks, 1 at a time, beating well after each addition. Stir in chocolate mixture and vanilla. Add flour mixture alternately with buttermilk, beating after each addition until smooth.

BEAT egg whites in another large bowl with electric mixer on high speed until they form stiff peaks. Gently stir into batter. Pour batter into prepared pans.

BAKE 30 minutes or until cake springs back when lightly touched in center. Immediately run spatula between cakes and sides of pans. Cool in pans 15 minutes. Remove from pans. Peel off waxed paper. Cool completely on wire racks.

SPREAD Classic Coconut-Pecan Filling and Frosting between layers and over top of cake.
Makes 12 servings

Hershey's introduced Hershey's Kisses Milk Chocolates in 1907, Hershey's Kisses with Almonds Chocolates in 1990, and Hershey's Hugs Chocolates and Hershey's Hugs with Almonds Chocolates in 1993.

Senior Hall of Milton Hershey School in the 1940s.
Photo courtesy of Hershey Foods Corporation

Hot Fudge Pudding Cake

1¼ cups granulated sugar, divided
1 cup all-purpose flour
7 tablespoons HERSHEY₀S Cocoa, divided
2 teaspoons baking powder
¼ teaspoon salt
½ cup milk
⅓ cup butter or margarine, melted
1½ teaspoons vanilla extract
½ cup packed light brown sugar
1¼ cups hot water
Whipped topping

Heat oven to 350°F. In bowl, stir together ¾ cup granulated sugar, flour, 3 tablespoons cocoa, baking powder and salt. Stir in milk, butter and vanilla; beat until smooth. Pour batter into 8- or 9-inch square baking pan. Stir together remaining ½ cup granulated sugar, brown sugar and remaining 4 tablespoons cocoa; sprinkle mixture evenly over batter. Pour hot water over top; do not stir. Bake 35 to 40 minutes or until center is almost set. Let stand 15 minutes; spoon into dessert dishes, spooning sauce from bottom of pan over top. Garnish with whipped topping, if desired.

Makes about 8 servings

Old-Fashioned Chocolate Cake

¾ cup (1½ sticks) butter or margarine, softened
1⅔ cups sugar
3 eggs
1 teaspoon vanilla extract
2 cups all-purpose flour
⅔ cup HERSHEY₍®₎S Cocoa
1¼ teaspoons baking soda
1 teaspoon salt
¼ teaspoon baking powder
1⅓ cups water
½ cup finely crushed hard peppermint candy (optional)
One-Bowl Buttercream Frosting (page 137)
Additional crushed hard peppermint candy (optional)

Heat oven to 350°F. Grease and flour two 9-inch round baking pans or one 13×9×2-inch baking pan. In large mixer bowl, combine butter, sugar, eggs and vanilla; beat on high speed of electric mixer 3 minutes. Stir together flour, cocoa, baking soda, salt and baking powder; add alternately with water to butter mixture. Blend just until combined; add candy, if desired. Pour batter into prepared pans. Bake 30 to 35 minutes or until wooden pick inserted in center comes out clean. Cool 10 minutes; remove from pans to wire racks. Cool completely. Frost with One-Bowl Buttercream Frosting. Just before serving, garnish with additional peppermint candy, if desired.   *Makes 8 to 10 servings*

Classic Coconut-Pecan Filling and Frosting

1 can (12 ounces) evaporated milk
1½ cups sugar
¾ cup (1½ sticks) butter or margarine
4 egg yolks, slightly beaten
1½ teaspoons vanilla
1 package (7 ounces) BAKER'S® ANGEL FLAKE® Coconut (about 2⅔ cups)
1½ cups chopped pecans

STIR milk, sugar, butter, egg yolks and vanilla in large saucepan. Cook over medium heat until mixture thickens and is golden brown, about 12 minutes, stirring constantly. Remove from heat.

STIR in coconut and pecans. Cool to room temperature and of spreading consistency.
Makes about 4½ cups or enough to fill and frost top of 1 (3-layer) cake, frost tops of 2 (13×9-inch) cakes or frost 24 cupcakes

Chocolate Mayonnaise Cake

2 cups all-purpose flour
⅔ cup unsweetened cocoa
1¼ teaspoons baking soda
¼ teaspoon baking powder
3 eggs
1⅔ cups sugar
1 teaspoon vanilla
1 cup HELLMANN'S® or BEST FOODS® Real or Light Mayonnaise or Low Fat Mayonnaise Dressing
1⅓ cups water

Chocolate Mayonnaise Cake

Grease and flour bottoms of two 9×1½-inch round cake pans. In medium bowl, combine flour, cocoa, baking soda and baking powder; set aside. In large bowl with mixer at high speed, beat eggs, sugar and vanilla, scraping bowl occasionally, 3 minutes or until smooth and creamy. Reduce speed to low; beat in mayonnaise until blended. Add flour mixture in 4 additions alternately with water, beginning and ending with flour mixture. Pour into prepared pans. Bake in 350°F oven 30 to 35 minutes or until cake springs back when touched lightly in center. Cool in pans on wire racks 10 minutes. Remove from pans; cool completely on racks. Fill and frost as desired.
Makes 1 (9-inch) layer cake

Chocolate Cream Torte

1 package DUNCAN HINES® Moist Deluxe Devil's Food Cake Mix
1 package (8 ounces) cream cheese, softened
½ cup sugar
1 teaspoon vanilla extract
1 cup finely chopped pecans
1 cup whipping cream, chilled
Strawberry halves, for garnish
Mint leaves, for garnish (optional)

1. Preheat oven to 350°F. Grease and flour two 8- or 9-inch round cake pans.

2. Prepare, bake and cool cake following package directions for basic recipe. Chill layers for ease in splitting.

3. Place cream cheese, sugar and vanilla extract in small bowl. Beat at low speed with electric mixer until smooth. Add pecans; stir until blended. Set aside. Beat whipping cream in small bowl until stiff peaks form. Fold whipped cream into cream cheese mixture.

4. To assemble, split each cake layer in half horizontally. Place one cake layer on serving plate. Spread top with one fourth of filling. Repeat with remaining layers and filling. Garnish with strawberry halves and mint leaves, if desired. Refrigerate until ready to serve.   *Makes 12 to 16 servings*

Mr. Duncan Hines (top photo), founder of Duncan Hines, was a famous traveling restaurant critic in the 1930s. Duncan Hines introduced its "New Fudge Marble Cake Mix" in 1957 (bottom photo).

Chocolate Cream Torte

Mott's® Marble Brownies

½ cup unsweetened cocoa powder
½ cup plus 2 tablespoons all-purpose
   flour, divided
1 teaspoon baking powder
½ teaspoon salt
2 tablespoons margarine
1½ cups plus ¼ cup granulated sugar,
   divided
3 egg whites, divided
½ cup MOTT'S® Natural Apple Sauce
1½ teaspoons vanilla extract, divided
4 ounces fat-free cream cheese

1. Preheat oven to 350°F. Spray 8-inch
square baking pan with nonstick cooking
spray.

2. In medium bowl, sift together cocoa
powder, ½ cup flour, baking powder and salt.

3. In large bowl, beat margarine and 1½ cups
sugar with electric mixer at medium speed
until blended. Whisk in 2 egg whites, apple
sauce and 1 teaspoon vanilla extract. Stir in
flour mixture until combined.

4. In small bowl, beat cream cheese and
¼ cup sugar with electric mixer at medium
speed until well blended. Stir in remaining
egg white, 2 tablespoons flour and ½
teaspoon vanilla extract.

5. Pour brownie mixture into prepared pan.
Spoon cream cheese mixture on top of
brownie mixture. Cut through both mixtures
with knife to create marbled design.

6. Bake 35 to 40 minutes or until firm. Cool
on wire rack 15 minutes; cut into 12 bars.
Makes 12 servings

Among the treasures *Columbus brought back to King Ferdinand were a few brown beans, probably cocoa beans. No one knew what to do with them until Cortes visited Mexico where he drank a brew made from such beans. The Aztecs called it "cacahuatl," or "gift from the gods." Cortes brought the chocolate back to Spain and eventually the drink was introduced to the rest of Europe. In 1765, an Irish immigrant, John Hannon, started milling chocolate in Dorchester, Massachusetts. Without the expensive import costs, the price went down and chocolate became a popular drink.*

One Bowl® Brownies

4 squares BAKER'S® Unsweetened
   Chocolate
¾ cup (1½ sticks) butter or margarine
2 cups sugar
3 eggs
1 teaspoon vanilla
1 cup flour
1 cup coarsely chopped nuts (optional)

One Bowl® Brownies

HEAT oven to 350°F (325°F for glass baking dish). Line 13×9-inch baking pan with foil extending over edges to form handles. Grease foil.

MICROWAVE chocolate and butter in large microwavable bowl on HIGH 2 minutes or until butter is melted. **Stir until chocolate is completely melted.**

STIR sugar into chocolate mixture until well blended. Mix in eggs and vanilla until well blended. Stir in flour and nuts until well blended. Spread in prepared pan.

BAKE for 30 to 35 minutes or until toothpick inserted into center comes out with fudgy crumbs. **DO NOT OVERBAKE.** Cool in pan. Lift out of pan onto cutting board. Cut into squares. *Makes about 24 brownies*

Tip

• For cakelike brownies, stir in ½ cup milk with eggs and vanilla. Increase flour to 1½ cups.

Double-Decker Fudge

1 cup REESE'S® Peanut Butter Chips
1 cup HERSHEY®S Semi-Sweet
    Chocolate Chips or HERSHEY®S
    MINI CHIPS® Semi-Sweet Chocolate
2¼ cups sugar
1 jar (7 ounces) marshmallow creme
¾ cup evaporated milk
¼ cup (½ stick) butter or margarine
1 teaspoon vanilla extract

Line 8-inch square pan with foil, extending foil over edges of pan. Measure peanut butter chips into one medium bowl and chocolate chips into second medium bowl. In heavy 3-quart saucepan, combine sugar, marshmallow creme, evaporated milk and butter. Cook over medium heat, stirring constantly, until mixture boils; boil and stir 5 minutes. Remove from heat; stir in vanilla. Immediately stir ½ of hot mixture (1½ cups) into peanut butter chips until chips are completely melted; quickly pour into prepared pan. Stir remaining ½ of hot mixture into chocolate chips until chips are completely melted. Quickly spread over top of peanut butter layer. Cool; refrigerate 1½ hours or until firm. Remove from pan; place on cutting board. Peel off foil; cut into 1-inch squares. Store tightly covered in refrigerator.
Makes about 5 dozen pieces or
about 2 pounds candy

Peanut Butter Fudge: Omit chocolate chips; place 1⅔ cups (10-ounce package) Reese's® Peanut Butter Chips in large bowl. Cook fudge mixture as directed above; add to chips, stirring until chips are completely melted. Pour into prepared pan; cool to room temperature.

Rich Cocoa Fudge

3 cups sugar
⅔ cup HERSHEY®S Cocoa or
    HERSHEY®S European Style Cocoa
⅛ teaspoon salt
1½ cups milk
¼ cup (½ stick) butter or margarine
1 teaspoon vanilla extract

Line 8- or 9-inch square pan with foil; butter foil. In heavy 4-quart saucepan, stir together sugar, cocoa and salt; stir in milk. Cook over medium heat, stirring constantly, until mixture comes to a full rolling boil. Boil, without stirring, to 234°F or until syrup, when dropped into very cold water, forms a soft ball which flattens when removed from water. (Bulb of candy thermometer should not rest on bottom of saucepan.) Remove from heat. Add butter and vanilla. DO NOT STIR. Cool at room temperature to 110°F (lukewarm). Beat with wooden spoon until fudge thickens and loses some of its gloss. Spread quickly into prepared pan; cool. Cut into squares.
Makes about 36 pieces or 1¾ pounds

Nutty Rich Cocoa Fudge: Beat cooked fudge as directed. Immediately stir in 1 cup chopped almonds, pecans or walnuts; quickly spread into prepared pan.

High Altitude Directions: Increase milk to 1⅔ cups. Use soft-ball cold water test for doneness or test and read thermometer in boiling water; subtract difference from 212°F. Then subtract that number from 234°F. This is the soft-ball temperature for your altitude and thermometer.

From left to right: Nutty Rich Cocoa Fudge
and Double-Decker Fudge

Carnation® Famous Fudge

2 tablespoons butter or margarine
⅔ cup undiluted CARNATION®
    Evaporated Milk
1½ cups granulated sugar
¼ teaspoon salt
2 cups (4 ounces) miniature
    marshmallows
1½ cups (9 ounces) NESTLÉ® TOLL
    HOUSE® Semi-Sweet Chocolate
    Morsels
½ cup chopped pecans or walnuts
1 teaspoon vanilla extract

COMBINE butter, evaporated milk, sugar and salt in medium, heavy saucepan. Bring to a boil over medium heat, stirring constantly. Boil 4 to 5 minutes, stirring constantly. Remove from heat.

STIR in marshmallows, morsels, nuts and vanilla. Stir vigorously 1 minute or until marshmallows are melted. Pour into foil-lined 8×8-inch baking pan; chill until firm. Cut into 1½×1½-inch squares.

Makes about 2 pounds

Milk Chocolate Fudge: Substitute 2 cups (11½-ounce package) Nestlé® Toll House® Milk Chocolate Morsels for Semi-Sweet Morsels.

Butterscotch Fudge: Substitute 2 cups (12-ounce package) Nestlé® Toll House® Butterscotch Flavored Morsels for Semi-Sweet Morsels.

Mint Chocolate Fudge: Substitute 1½ cups (10-ounce package) Nestlé® Toll House® Mint Flavored Chocolate Morsels for Semi-Sweet Morsels.

Carnation

Your Grocery Boy
will deliver
Carnation Milk
FROM CONTENTED COWS

Nestlé Food Company opened a brand new plant in 1993 to meet demands of a market that consumes 10 million cases of evaporated milk each year.

Foolproof Dark Chocolate Fudge

3 cups (18 ounces) semi-sweet chocolate chips
1 (14-ounce) can EAGLE® BRAND Sweetened Condensed Milk (NOT evaporated milk)
Dash salt
1 cup chopped nuts
1½ teaspoons vanilla extract

In large heavy saucepan, over low heat, melt chips with sweetened condensed milk and salt, stirring frequently until smooth. Remove from heat; stir in nuts and vanilla. Spread evenly into aluminum foil-lined tree-shaped mold or 9-inch square pan. Chill 2 hours or until firm. Place fudge on cutting board; peel off foil. Garnish as desired or cut into squares. Store loosely covered at room temperature.   *Makes about 2 pounds*

Microwave: In 1-quart glass measure with handle, combine chips with sweetened condensed milk and salt. Cook on HIGH 3 minutes or until chips melt, stirring after each 1½ minutes. Stir in nuts and vanilla. Proceed as above.

Tip: For ease in cutting fudge and cleaning pan, line pan with foil before preparing fudge; lightly grease foil. When fudge has cooled, lift from pan; cut fudge into squares.

Peanut Butter Fudge Sauce

½ cup KARO® Light or Dark Corn Syrup
½ cup SKIPPY® Creamy Peanut Butter
¼ cup heavy or whipping cream
½ cup semisweet chocolate chips

In 1½-quart microwavable bowl combine corn syrup, peanut butter and cream. Microwave on HIGH 1½ minutes or until boiling. Add chocolate chips; stir until melted. Serve warm over ice cream. Store in refrigerator.
Makes about 1¼ cups

Note: To reheat, microwave uncovered on LOW (30%) about 1½ minutes, just until pourable.

One-Bowl Buttercream Frosting

6 tablespoons butter or margarine, softened
2⅔ cups powdered sugar
½ cup HERSHEY'S Cocoa
⅓ cup milk
1 teaspoon vanilla extract

In small mixer bowl, beat butter. Add powdered sugar and cocoa alternately with milk; beat to spreading consistency (additional milk may be needed). Blend in vanilla.   *Makes about 2 cups frosting*

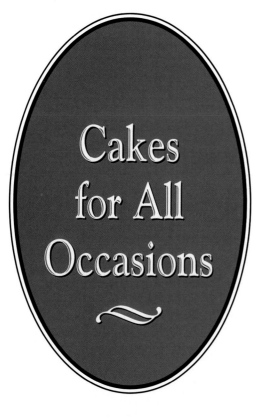

Cakes
for All
Occasions

Make every occasion special with scrumptious cakes and cheesecakes suitable for festive birthday parties, family holidays, special dinner parties or casual gatherings.

Carrot Layer Cake

Cake

　　1 package DUNCAN HINES® Moist
　　　　Deluxe Yellow Cake Mix
　　4 eggs
　　½ cup CRISCO® Oil or CRISCO®
　　　　PURITAN® Canola Oil
　　3 cups grated carrots
　　1 cup finely chopped nuts
　　2 teaspoons ground cinnamon

Cream Cheese Frosting

　　1 (8-ounce) package cream cheese,
　　　　softened
　　¼ cup butter or margarine, softened
　　2 teaspoons vanilla extract
　　4 cups confectioners sugar

1. Preheat oven to 350°F. Grease and flour 2 (8- or 9-inch) round baking pans.

2. **For cake,** combine cake mix, eggs, oil, carrots, nuts and cinnamon in large bowl. Beat at low speed with electric mixer until moistened. Beat at medium speed for 2 minutes. Pour into pans. Bake at 350°F for 35 to 40 minutes or until toothpick inserted in centers comes out clean. Cool.

3. **For frosting,** place cream cheese, butter and vanilla extract in large bowl. Beat at low speed until smooth and creamy. Add confectioners sugar gradually, beating until smooth. Add more sugar to thicken or milk or water to thin frosting, as needed. Fill and frost cooled cake. Garnish with whole pecans.　　　*Makes 12 to 16 servings*

Carrot Layer Cake

Cappuccino Cake

½ cup (3 ounces) chocolate chips
½ cup chopped hazelnuts, walnuts or
　　pecans
1 (18.25-ounce) package yellow cake
　　mix
¼ cup instant espresso coffee powder
2 teaspoons ground cinnamon
1¼ cups water
3 eggs
⅓ cup FILIPPO BERIO® Pure or Extra
　　Light Tasting Olive Oil
　　Powdered sugar
1 (15-ounce) container ricotta cheese
2 teaspoons granulated sugar
　　Additional ground cinnamon

Preheat oven to 325°F. Grease 10-inch
(12-cup) Bundt pan or 10-inch tube pan
with olive oil. Sprinkle lightly with flour.

In small bowl, combine chocolate chips and
hazelnuts. Spoon evenly into bottom of
prepared pan.

In large bowl, combine cake mix, coffee
powder and 2 teaspoons cinnamon. Add
water, eggs and olive oil. Beat with electric
mixer at low speed until dry ingredients are
moistened. Beat at medium speed 2 minutes.
Pour batter over topping in pan.

Bake 60 minutes or until toothpick inserted in
center comes out clean. Cool on wire rack 15
minutes. Remove from pan. Place cake,
fluted side up, on serving plate. Cool
completely. Sprinkle with powdered sugar.

In rnedium bowl, combine ricotta cheese and
granulated sugar. Sprinkle with additional
cinnamon. Serve alongside slices of cake.
Serve with cappuccino, espresso or your
favorite coffee, if desired.
Makes 12 to 16 servings

Olive Oil Pound Cake

2¼ cups all-purpose flour
1¼ teaspoons salt
1 teaspoon baking powder
¾ cup FILIPPO BERIO® Extra Light
　　Tasting Olive Oil
1½ cups sugar
2 tablespoons orange juice
2 teaspoons vanilla
3 eggs
⅔ cup milk

Preheat oven to 325°F. Grease 2
(6¾×3½-inch) loaf pans with olive oil.

In medium bowl, combine flour, salt and
baking powder.

In large bowl, place olive oil. Slowly beat in
sugar, orange juice and vanilla with electric
mixer at medium speed until blended. Add
eggs, one at a time, beating well after each
addition. Add milk; beat 2 minutes. Gradually
beat flour mixture into olive oil mixture until
well blended. Pour batter equally into
prepared pans.

Bake 50 to 55 minutes or until golden brown
and toothpick inserted in centers comes out
clean. Cool on wire racks 15 minutes.
Remove from pans; cool completely on wire
racks. *Makes 2 small loaves*

Cappuccino Cake

Grandma's Favorite Molasses Fruitcake

**2 California-Arizona oranges
1 cup light molasses
1 package (15 ounces) raisins
1 package (8 ounces) dates, chopped
2 containers (16 ounces each) glacé
     fruit mix
1¼ cups granulated sugar
1 cup butter or margarine, softened
6 eggs
3 cups all-purpose flour
1½ teaspoons ground cinnamon
1 teaspoon baking soda
1 teaspoon ground nutmeg
½ teaspoon ground allspice
½ teaspoon ground cloves
1 cup freshly squeezed orange juice
2 cups nut halves
     Powdered sugar**

Cut oranges into large chunks. In blender or food processor, finely chop oranges to measure 1⅓ cups. In large saucepan, combine chopped oranges, molasses, raisins and dates; bring to a boil. Reduce heat and simmer 5 to 10 minutes. Remove from heat; stir in fruit mix. Set aside.

Preheat oven to 300°F. In large bowl, cream together sugar and butter. Beat in eggs, one at a time. Sift together flour, cinnamon, baking soda, nutmeg, allspice and cloves. Add to creamed mixture alternately with orange juice. Stir batter into molasses-fruit mixture. Add nuts. Divide batter; spoon 8 cups batter into *well-greased* 10-inch Bundt or tube pan. With remaining 6 cups batter, make 2 dozen cupcakes *or* 8 dozen mini fruitcakes. Bake 2 hours or until toothpick inserted in center comes out clean. Cool 10

minutes. Remove from pan; cool on wire rack. To serve, sprinkle with powdered sugar. Garnish with orange pieces and candied cherries, if desired.

Favorite recipe from **Sunkist Growers**

Western Golden Fruitcake

**1 cup butter or margarine, softened
2 cups sugar
4 eggs
4 cups all-purpose flour
1½ teaspoons baking soda
1 cup buttermilk
½ cup freshly squeezed orange juice
2 cups pecan or walnut halves
1 package (8 ounces) dates, chopped
8 ounces candied cherries, halved
8 ounces candied pineapple chunks
     Grated peel of 2 fresh oranges
     Fresh Orange Glaze or Fresh Lemon
     Glaze (recipes follow)**

Preheat oven to 300°F. In large bowl, cream together butter and sugar. Beat in eggs, one at a time. Sift together flour and baking soda. Add to creamed mixture alternately with buttermilk and orange juice, beating until smooth. Stir in nuts, dates, cherries, pineapple and orange peel. Divide batter; spoon 7½ cups into *well-greased* 10-inch Bundt or tube pan and spoon remaining 2½ cups batter into *well-greased* 7½×3½×2¼-inch loaf pan. Bake both cakes 2 hours or until toothpick inserted in center comes out clean. Cool 10 minutes. Remove from pans; cool on wire racks. To serve, drizzle cakes with Fresh Orange Glaze or Fresh Lemon Glaze and garnish with nut halves, if desired.

Fresh Orange Glaze: In small bowl, combine 1 cup confectioners' sugar, 1 teaspoon freshly grated orange peel and 1½ to 2 tablespoons freshly squeezed orange juice.

Fresh Lemon Glaze: In small bowl, combine 1 cup confectioners' sugar, 1 teaspoon freshly grated lemon peel and 1½ to 2 tablespoons freshly squeezed lemon juice.

Favorite recipe from **Sunkist Growers**

Holiday Fruit Cake

  1 (16-ounce) package HONEY MAID®
      Grahams, finely rolled (about
      5 cups crumbs)
½ teaspoon ground cinnamon
½ teaspoon ground allspice
¼ teaspoon ground cloves
¾ cup seedless raisins
  1 cup pitted dates, snipped
12 ounces mixed candied fruit
      (about 1½ cups)
  1 cup PLANTERS® Walnut Pieces,
      chopped
½ cup orange juice
⅓ cup light corn syrup

In large bowl, combine crumbs, cinnamon, allspice, cloves, raisins, dates, candied fruit and walnuts. Stir together orange juice and corn syrup; add to crumb mixture, blending until moistened. Press firmly into foil-lined 8½×4½×2½-inch loaf pan; cover tightly. Store at least 2 days in refrigerator before serving. Cake will keep several weeks in refrigerator.   *Makes 1 (8-inch) loaf*

PLANTERS® *Amedeo Obici immigrated to Pennsylvania from his native Italy at the young age of 12. At the age of 19, he opened a fruit stand that also had a peanut roaster. He developed a system to turn the roaster automatically instead of by hand and also conceived the idea of salting the peanuts to enhance the flavor. In 1906, in partnership with a fellow immigrant, Mario Peruzzi, the Planters Nut & Chocolate Company was formed. In 1916, as a way to enhance the popularity of the peanut, the partners offered a prize for the best sketch suitable for the company trademark. The winning design, an animated peanut, was submitted by a schoolboy. Later a commercial artist added a top hat, monocle and cane, and Mr. Peanut was born.*

Flag Cake

2 pints strawberries
1 package (12 ounces) pound cake, cut into 8 slices
1⅓ cups blueberries, divided
1 tub (8 ounces) COOL WHIP Whipped Topping, thawed

SLICE 1 cup strawberries; set aside. Halve remaining strawberries; set aside.

LINE bottom of 12×8-inch baking dish with cake slices. Top with 1 cup sliced strawberries, 1 cup blueberries and all of whipped topping.

PLACE strawberry halves and remaining ⅓ cup blueberries over whipped topping to create a flag design.

REFRIGERATE until ready to serve.

Makes 15 servings

Flag Cake

Mott's® Pineapple Upside Down Cake

1 (8-ounce) can crushed pineapple in juice, undrained
2 tablespoons margarine, melted and divided
½ cup packed light brown sugar
6 whole maraschino cherries
1½ cups all-purpose flour
2 tablespoons baking powder
¼ teaspoon salt
1 cup granulated sugar
½ cup MOTT'S® Natural Apple Sauce
1 whole egg
3 egg whites, beaten until stiff

1. Preheat oven to 375°F. Spray 8×8-inch baking pan with nonstick cooking spray. Drain pineapple; reserve juice.

2. Spread 1 tablespoon melted margarine evenly in bottom of prepared pan. Sprinkle with brown sugar; top with pineapple. Slice cherries in half. Arrange cherries, cut side up, so that when cake is cut, each piece will have cherry half in center.

3. In small bowl, combine flour, baking powder and salt. In large bowl, combine granulated sugar, apple sauce, whole egg, remaining 1 tablespoon melted margarine and reserved pineapple juice.

4. Add flour mixture to apple sauce mixture; stir until well blended. Fold in egg whites. Gently pour batter over fruit, spreading evenly.

5. Bake 35 to 40 minutes or until lightly browned. Cool on wire rack 10 minutes. Invert cake onto serving plate. Serve warm or cool completely. Cut into 12 pieces.

Makes 12 servings

Cookies 'n' Cream Cheesecake

**1 cup chocolate sandwich cookie
crumbs (about 12 cookies)**
1 tablespoon margarine, melted
**3 (8-ounce) packages PHILADELPHIA
BRAND® Cream Cheese, softened**
1 cup sugar
2 tablespoons all-purpose flour
1 teaspoon vanilla
3 eggs
**1 cup coarsely chopped chocolate
sandwich cookies (about 8 cookies)**

• Preheat oven to 325°F.

• Mix together crumbs and margarine in small
bowl. Press onto bottom of 9-inch springform
pan. Bake 10 minutes.

• Beat cream cheese, sugar, flour and vanilla
in large mixing bowl at medium speed with
electric mixer until well blended.

• Add eggs, one at a time, mixing well after
each addition. Fold in chopped cookies. Pour
over crust.

• Bake 1 hour and 5 minutes. Loosen cake
from rim of pan; cool before removing rim of
pan. Chill. Garnish with thawed COOL
WHIP® Whipped Topping, chocolate
sandwich cookies, cut in half, and mint
leaves, if desired.

Makes 10 to 12 servings

*Cream cheese was
developed over
100 years ago
and was first produced commercially
by an ambitious, hard-working farmer
in upstate New York. It was primarily
used as a flavorful spread for bread,
toast or crackers. This fresh, delicate
cheese was not used as a recipe
ingredient until the mid-1920s. One of
the first recipes developed was the
"Kraft Philadelphia Cream Cake,"
which was later retitled "Supreme
Cheesecake." This recipe became an
instant favorite and what began as a
novel idea—cooking with cream
cheese—has become a universally
accepted concept. Today, Philadelphia
Brand Cream Cheese is an
indispensable ingredient used by
great American cooks like you.*

Cookies 'n' Cream Cheesecake

Cocoa Cheesecake

2 packages (8 ounces each) cream cheese, softened
¾ cup plus 2 tablespoons sugar, divided
½ cup HERSHEY₅S Cocoa
2 teaspoons vanilla extract, divided
2 eggs
  Graham Crust (recipe follows)
1 cup (8 ounces) dairy sour cream
  Fresh fruit, sliced

Heat oven to 375°F. In large mixer bowl, beat cream cheese, ¾ cup sugar, cocoa and 1 teaspoon vanilla until well blended. Add eggs; blend well. Pour batter into prepared Graham Crust. Bake 20 minutes. Remove from oven; cool 15 minutes. *Increase oven temperature to 425°F.* In small bowl, stir together sour cream, remaining 2 tablespoons sugar and remaining 1 teaspoon vanilla until smooth; spread evenly over top of cheesecake. Bake 10 minutes; remove from oven. Loosen cheesecake from side of pan; cool to room temperature. Refrigerate several hours or overnight; remove side of pan. Garnish with fresh fruit. Cover; refrigerate leftover cheesecake.   *Makes 10 to 12 servings*

Graham Crust: In bowl, combine 1½ cups graham cracker crumbs, ⅓ cup sugar and ⅓ cup melted butter or margarine. Press mixture onto bottom and halfway up side of 9-inch springform pan.

Variation:

Chocolate Lover's Cheesecake: Prepare batter as directed above; stir 1 cup Hershey₅s Semi-Sweet Chocolate Chips into batter before pouring into crust. Bake and serve as directed.

Philly 3-Step™ Cheesecake

2 (8-ounce) packages PHILADELPHIA BRAND® Cream Cheese or PHILADELPHIA BRAND® Neufchâtel Cheese, ⅓ Less Fat Than Cream Cheese, softened
½ cup sugar
½ teaspoon vanilla
2 eggs
1 prepared graham cracker crumb crust (6 ounces or 9 inches)

1. MIX cream cheese, sugar and vanilla with electric mixer on medium speed until well blended. Add eggs; mix until blended.

2. POUR into crust.

3. BAKE at 350°F for 40 minutes or until center is almost set. Cool. Refrigerate 3 hours or overnight.   *Makes 8 servings*

Historical ad promoting Nabisco's® Vanilla Wafers.

Individual Cherry Cheesecakes

12 NILLA® Wafers
2 (8-ounce) packages cream cheese, softened
¾ cup sugar
2 eggs
Cherry pie filling

Place 1 wafer in bottom of each of 12 (2½-inch) paper-lined muffin-pan cups; set aside.

In large bowl, with electric mixer at medium speed, beat cream cheese, sugar and eggs until light and fluffy. Spoon filling into each cup, filling about ⅔ full.

Bake at 350°F for 30 minutes. Turn off oven; open door slightly. Let cool in oven for 30 minutes. Remove from oven; cool completely. Top with pie filling. Chill at least 1 hour.

Makes 12 servings

Marble Cheesecake

Chocolate Crumb Crust (recipe follows)
3 packages (8 ounces each) cream cheese, softened
1 cup sugar, divided
½ cup dairy sour cream
2½ teaspoons vanilla extract, divided
3 tablespoons all-purpose flour
3 eggs
¼ cup HERSHEY'S Cocoa
1 tablespoon vegetable oil

Prepare Chocolate Crumb Crust. Heat oven to 450°F. In large mixer bowl, beat cream cheese, ¾ cup sugar, sour cream and 2 teaspoons vanilla until smooth. Gradually add flour, blending well. Add eggs, one at a time, beating well after each addition; set aside. Stir together cocoa and remaining ¼ cup sugar. Add oil, remaining ½ teaspoon vanilla and 1½ cups cream cheese mixture; blend well. Spoon plain and chocolate batters alternately over prepared Chocolate Crumb Crust, ending with spoonfuls of chocolate on top; gently swirl with spatula or knife for marbled effect. Bake 10 minutes. *Reduce oven temperature to 250°F;* continue baking 30 minutes. Turn off oven; leave cheesecake in oven 30 minutes without opening door. Remove from oven. Loosen cheesecake from side of pan; cool to room temperature. Refrigerate several hours or overnight; remove side of pan. Cover; refrigerate leftover cheesecake.

Makes 10 to 12 servings

Chocolate Crumb Crust: Heat oven to 350°F. In bowl, stir together 1¼ cups vanilla wafer crumbs, ⅓ cup powdered sugar and ⅓ cup Hershey's Cocoa; blend in ¼ cup (½ stick) butter or margarine, melted. Press mixture onto bottom and ½ inch up side of 9-inch springform pan. Bake 8 minutes; cool completely.

Classic Sour Cream Cheesecake

Classic Sour Cream Cheesecake

1½ cups shortbread cookie crumbs
    (about 24 cookies)
 2 tablespoons margarine or butter,
    melted
 3 (8-ounce) packages cream cheese,
    softened
 1 (14-ounce) can EAGLE® Brand
    Sweetened Condensed Milk
    (NOT evaporated milk)
 4 eggs
 1 (8-ounce) container BORDEN® or
    MEADOW GOLD® Sour Cream
 1 tablespoon vanilla extract

Preheat oven to 350°. Combine crumbs and margarine; press firmly on bottom of 9-inch springform pan. In large mixer bowl, beat cheese until fluffy. Gradually beat in sweetened condensed milk until smooth. Beat in eggs then sour cream and vanilla. Pour into prepared pan. Bake 50 to 55 minutes or until lightly browned around edge (center will be slightly soft). Cool. Chill. Just before serving, remove side of springform pan. Garnish with cherry pie filling, if desired. Refrigerate leftovers.

Makes one 9-inch cheesecake

Creamy Strawberry Cheesecake

½ cup **NABISCO® Graham Cracker Crumbs**
1 cup sugar
2 tablespoons margarine, melted
1 (24-ounce) container lowfat cottage cheese (1% milkfat)
2 cups **EGG BEATERS® Real Egg Product**
2 (8-ounce) packages light cream cheese (Neufchâtel), softened
½ teaspoon almond extract (optional)
2 cups sliced strawberries
Mint sprig, for garnish

In small bowl, combine crumbs, 2 tablespoons sugar and margarine; press on bottom of 9-inch springform pan. Set aside.

In electric blender or food processor, purée cottage cheese and ½ cup egg product, scraping down side of container as necessary. In large bowl, with mixer at high speed, beat cream cheese, ¾ cup sugar, cottage cheese mixture, almond extract and remaining 1½ cups egg product until smooth; pour over crust in pan.

Bake at 325°F for 1 hour or until puffed and set. Cool on rack 15 minutes. Carefully run metal spatula around edge of cheesecake to loosen. Chill at least 3 hours.

In electric blender, purée 1 cup strawberries and remaining 2 tablespoons sugar. Arrange remaining 1 cup strawberries on cheesecake; drizzle with strawberry purée. Chill until serving time. Garnish with mint sprig.

Makes 16 servings

During the last century, Sylvester Graham, an ordained Presbyterian minister, rose to fame for his touting of unsifted, coarsely ground wheat flour. In 1829, he invented the graham cracker, made from coarsely ground graham flour. It was the National Biscuit Company (forerunner of Nabisco, Inc.) that was able to convert Graham's invention to mass production. Choice winter wheat berries are ground to just the right size to give the cracker its distinctive flavor and texture. Molasses is added for flavor and golden color, creating a perfect snack with wholesome taste made from natural ingredients.

Old-Fashioned Pies & Desserts

Create delightful new memories for family and friends by topping off a meal with one of these treasured recipes.

Traditional Cherry Pie

3 cups frozen tart cherries
1 cup granulated sugar
2 tablespoons quick-cooking tapioca
½ teaspoon almond extract
Pastry for 2-crust, 9-inch pie
2 tablespoons butter or margarine

Preheat oven to 400°F.

In medium bowl, combine cherries, sugar, tapioca and almond extract; mix well. (It is not necessary to thaw cherries before using.) Let cherry mixture stand 15 minutes.

Line 9-inch pie plate with pastry; fill with cherry mixture. Dot with butter. Cover with top crust, cutting slits for steam to escape.

Bake 50 to 55 minutes, or until crust is golden brown and filling is bubbly.
Makes 6 to 8 servings

Favorite recipe from **Cherry Marketing Institute, Inc.**

Traditional Cherry Pie

Elegant and Easy Pear Tart

Elegant and Easy Pear Tart

1 can (29 ounces) Bartlett pears
2 packages (3⅛ to 3½ ounces each)
   vanilla pudding mix
Milk
¼ cup almond-flavor liqueur*
1 (8-inch) pastry shell, baked and
   cooled
Apricot Glaze (recipe follows)

*One-half teaspoon almond extract can be substituted.

Drain pears; reserve 1 cup liquid. Prepare pudding according to package directions substituting reserved pear liquid for part of milk; stir in liqueur. Pour into pastry shell; chill until set. Slice pears and arrange over pudding. Brush with warm Apricot Glaze; refrigerate until cold.

Makes 1 (8-inch) tart

Apricot Glaze: Heat ½ cup apricot or peach preserves and 1 tablespoon almond-flavor liqueur or pear liquid. Press through sieve; discard pulp. Makes about ⅓ cup.

*Favorite recipe from **Pacific Coast Canned Pear Service***

Freestyle Apple Pie

    Crumb Topping (recipe follows)
 ½ cup sugar
 1 tablespoon ARGO® or KINGSFORD'S®
    Corn Starch
 ½ teaspoon cinnamon
 4 cups peeled, sliced apples (about
    4 medium)
 1 tablespoon lemon juice
 1 refrigerated prepared pie crust for
    9-inch pie

Prepare Crumb Topping; set aside. In large bowl combine sugar, corn starch and cinnamon. Add apples and lemon juice; toss to coat. Unfold crust; place on foil-lined cookie sheet. Spoon apples into center of crust, leaving 2-inch edge. Sprinkle Crumb Topping over apples. Fold up edge of crust, pinching at 2-inch intervals. Bake in 400°F oven 15 minutes. *Reduce temperature to 350°F;* bake 35 minutes longer or until apples are tender.   *Makes 6 servings*

Crumb Topping: In small bowl combine ½ cup flour and ⅓ cup packed brown sugar. With pastry blender or 2 knives, cut in ½ cup cold MAZOLA® Margarine just until coarse crumbs form.

Fourth of July Cherry Pie

 5 cups Northwest fresh sweet cherries,
    pitted
 2 tablespoons cornstarch
    Pastry for 2-crust (9-inch) pie
 2 tablespoons butter or margarine
 ⅓ cup sifted powdered sugar
 1 tablespoon fresh lemon juice
 1 teaspoon grated lemon peel

Preheat oven to 425°F. Sprinkle cornstarch over cherries; toss to coat. Turn into pastry-lined 9-inch pie pan. Dot with butter. Roll remaining pastry into 10-inch circle. Cut into ¾-inch-wide strips. Arrange lattice-fashion over filling; seal and flute edges. Bake 35 to 45 minutes or until filling bubbles. Combine powdered sugar, lemon juice and peel; drizzle over warm pie.   *Makes one 9-inch pie*

*Favorite recipe from **Northwest Cherry Growers***

Chilean Raspberry and Blueberry Pie

    Pastry for 2-crust, 9-inch pie
    (homemade or prepared)
 1⅓ cups plus 1 teaspoon sugar
 7 tablespoons cornstarch
 1 tablespoon grated orange peel
 4 cups Chilean raspberries
 2 cups Chilean blueberries
 1 tablespoon orange liqueur *or*
    ½ teaspoon grated orange peel

Preheat oven to 375°F. Line 9-inch pie pan with pastry. Mix 1⅓ cups sugar, cornstarch and orange peel in bowl; add raspberries, blueberries and orange liqueur. Mix well and pour into pie shell. Cover with top crust. Seal edges and flute or press together with tines of fork. Cut slits for steam to escape. Brush lightly with cold water; sprinkle with remaining 1 teaspoon sugar. Bake until top is golden brown, about 50 minutes. Let cool before serving with slightly sweetened whipped cream.   *Makes 8 servings*

*Favorite recipe from **Chilean Fresh Fruit Association***

Libby's® Famous Pumpkin Pie

1 unbaked 9-inch pie crust
2 eggs
1 can (16 ounces) LIBBY'S® Solid Pack Pumpkin
1½ cups (12-ounce can) undiluted CARNATION® Evaporated Milk
¾ cup granulated sugar
1 teaspoon ground cinnamon
½ teaspoon salt
½ teaspoon ground ginger
¼ teaspoon ground cloves

PREHEAT oven to 425°F.

LINE 9-inch pie plate with crust; decorate edge as desired. Beat eggs lightly in large bowl. Stir in pumpkin, milk, sugar, cinnamon, salt, ginger and cloves; pour into pie crust.

BAKE 15 minutes. *Reduce temperature to 350°F;* bake 40 to 50 minutes or until knife inserted near center comes out clean. Cool on wire rack.   *Makes one 9-inch pie*

Festive Pumpkin Pie

Flaky Pastry Crust (recipe follows)
1 (30-ounce) can pumpkin pie filling
⅔ cup undiluted evaporated milk
½ cup EGG BEATERS® Real Egg Product
Nondairy prepared whipped topping, for garnish
Orange peel, for garnish

Prepare Flaky Pastry Crust. In large bowl, whisk pie filling, evaporated milk and egg product until well blended. Pour into prepared crust. Bake at 425°F for 15 minutes. *Reduce*

oven temperature to 350°F. Bake 50 to 60 minutes more or until knife inserted 2 inches from center comes out clean. Cool completely. Garnish, if desired.
                    Makes 10 servings

Flaky Pastry Crust: Cut ⅓ cup margarine into 1¼ cups all-purpose flour until crumbly. Add 3 to 4 tablespoons ice water, one tablespoon at a time, until moistened. Shape into ball. Roll out to fit 9-inch pie plate. Transfer to plate; trim pastry and pinch to form high fluted edge.

Carnation

In 1899, E. A. Stuart and Thomas E. Yerxa, helped by a Swiss gentleman by the name of Meyerberg, developed a revolutionary method of evaporating milk without the addition of sugar. On the opening day of their factory, 2,744 quarts of fresh milk were condensed to 55 cases of evaporated milk.

Maple Pecan Pie

Maple Pecan Pie

1 (9-inch) unbaked pastry shell
1 cup CARY'S®, MAPLE ORCHARDS® or
MACDONALD'S™ Pure Maple Syrup
3 eggs, beaten
½ cup firmly packed light brown sugar
2 tablespoons margarine or butter,
melted
1 teaspoon vanilla extract
1¼ cups pecan halves or pieces

Place oven rack in lowest position in oven; preheat oven to 350°. In large bowl, combine all ingredients except pastry shell. Pour into pastry shell. Bake 35 to 40 minutes or until golden. Cool. Serve at room temperature or chilled. Refrigerate leftovers.

Makes one 9-inch pie

ReaLemon® Meringue Pie

1 (9-inch) baked pastry shell
1⅔ cups sugar
6 tablespoons cornstarch
½ cup REALEMON® Lemon Juice from Concentrate
4 eggs, separated
1½ cups boiling water
2 tablespoons margarine or butter
¼ teaspoon cream of tartar

Preheat oven to 300°. In heavy saucepan, combine 1⅓ cups sugar and cornstarch; add ReaLemon® brand. In small bowl, beat egg *yolks;* add to lemon mixture.

Gradually add water, stirring constantly. Over medium heat, cook and stir until mixture boils and thickens, about 8 to 10 minutes. Remove from heat. Add margarine; stir until melted. Pour into prepared pastry shell. In small mixer bowl, beat egg *whites* with cream of tartar until soft peaks form; gradually add remaining ⅓ cup sugar, beating until stiff but not dry. Spread on top of pie, sealing carefully to edge of shell. Bake 20 to 30 minutes or until golden. Cool. Chill before serving. Refrigerate leftovers.

Makes one 9-inch pie

ReaLime® Meringue Pie: Substitute ReaLime® Lime Juice from Concentrate for ReaLemon® brand. Add green food coloring to filling if desired. Proceed as above.

Creamy Key Lime Tart

Crust

3 cups HONEY ALMOND DELIGHT® brand cereal, crushed to 1½ cups
¼ cup packed brown sugar
¼ cup (½ stick) margarine or butter, melted

Filling

8 ounces cream cheese, softened
1 can (14 ounces) sweetened condensed milk
⅓ cup lime juice
1 teaspoon freshly grated lime peel
2 drops green food coloring (optional)
1 cup nondairy whipped topping

To prepare Crust: Preheat oven to 350°F. In medium bowl combine cereal, sugar and margarine; mix well. Press cereal mixture firmly onto bottom and sides of ungreased 9-inch fluted tart pan or 9-inch pie plate. Bake 8 to 9 minutes or until lightly browned. Cool completely.

To prepare Filling: In large bowl beat cream cheese and milk. Slowly add juice, peel and food coloring, if desired, beating until smooth. Fold in whipped topping. Pour evenly into cooled crust. Chill 1 hour or until set. Garnish with additional lime peel and whipped topping, if desired. *Makes 9 servings*

ReaLemon® Meringue Pie

Cool 'n Easy Pie

⅔ cup boiling water
1 package (4-serving size) JELL-O Brand Gelatin Dessert, any flavor
½ cup cold water
   Ice cubes
1 tub (8 ounces) COOL WHIP Whipped Topping, thawed
1 prepared graham cracker crumb crust (6 ounces)
   Assorted fruit (optional)

STIR boiling water into gelatin in large bowl 2 minutes or until completely dissolved. Mix cold water and ice to make 1¼ cups. Add to gelatin, stirring until slightly thickened. Remove any remaining ice.

STIR in whipped topping with wire whisk until smooth. Refrigerate 10 to 15 minutes or until mixture is very thick and will mound. Spoon into crust.

REFRIGERATE 4 hours or until firm. Just before serving, garnish with fruit, if desired. Store leftover pie in refrigerator.

Makes 8 servings

Ritz® Mock Apple Pie

Pastry for two-crust 9-inch pie
36 RITZ® Crackers, coarsely broken (about 1¾ cups crumbs)
1¾ cups water
2 cups sugar
2 teaspoons cream of tartar
2 tablespoons lemon juice
   Grated rind of 1 lemon
2 tablespoons margarine
½ teaspoon ground cinnamon

Roll out half of pastry and line 9-inch pie plate. Place cracker crumbs in prepared crust. In saucepan, over high heat, heat water, sugar and cream of tartar to a boil; simmer 15 minutes. Add lemon juice and rind; cool. Pour syrup over cracker crumbs. Dot with margarine; sprinkle with cinnamon. Roll out remaining pastry; place over pie. Trim, seal and flute edges. Slit top crust to allow steam to escape.

Bake at 425°F for 30 to 35 minutes or until crust is crisp and golden. Serve warm or let cool completely before serving.

Makes 10 servings

Historical ad for the "dessert that can be made in a minute."

Cool 'n Easy Pies

Coconut Lime Pie

1 (9-inch) baked pastry shell or graham cracker crumb crust
1 cup water
¼ cup cornstarch
3 tablespoons REALIME® Lime Juice from Concentrate
4 eggs, separated*
1 (15-ounce) can COCO LOPEZ® Cream of Coconut
¼ teaspoon cream of tartar
6 tablespoons sugar
2 tablespoons flaked coconut

*Use only Grade A clean, uncracked eggs.

Preheat oven to 350°. In heavy saucepan, combine water, cornstarch and ReaLime® brand; mix well. In small bowl, beat egg yolks; add to lime mixture. Add cream of coconut; mix well. Over medium heat, cook and stir until mixture boils and thickens, about 12 to 15 minutes. Pour into prepared pastry shell. In small mixer bowl, beat egg whites with cream of tartar to form soft peaks; gradually add sugar, beating until stiff but not dry. Spread on top of pie, sealing carefully to edge of pastry shell. Top with coconut. Bake 12 to 15 minutes or until golden. Cool. Chill. Refrigerate leftovers.

Makes one 9-inch pie

Tip: 1 cup (½ pint) BORDEN® or MEADOW GOLD® Whipping Cream, whipped, *or* 1 (4-ounce) container frozen nondairy whipped topping (1¾ cups), thawed, can be substituted for meringue (omit egg whites, sugar and cream of tartar). Cool pie to room temperature before topping with whipped cream. Chill before serving.

Classic Crisco® Crust

8-, 9- or 10-inch Single Crust
  1⅓ cups all-purpose flour
  ½ teaspoon salt
  ½ cup CRISCO® Shortening
  3 tablespoons cold water

8- or 9-inch Double Crust
  2 cups all-purpose flour
  1 teaspoon salt
  ¾ cup CRISCO® Shortening
  5 tablespoons cold water

10-inch Double Crust
  2⅔ cups all-purpose flour
  1 teaspoon salt
  1 cup CRISCO® Shortening
  7 to 8 tablespoons cold water

1. Spoon flour into measuring cup and level. Combine flour and salt in medium bowl.

2. Cut in Crisco® using pastry blender (or 2 knives) until all flour is blended to form pea-size chunks.

3. Sprinkle with water, 1 tablespoon at a time. Toss lightly with fork until dough forms a ball.

For Single Crust Pies
1. Press dough between hands to form 5- to 6-inch "pancake." Flour rolling surface and rolling pin lightly. Roll dough into circle.

2. Trim 1 inch larger than upside-down pie plate. Loosen dough carefully.

3. Fold dough into quarters. Unfold and press into pie plate. Fold edge under. Flute.

For Baked Pie Crusts
1. For recipes using baked pie crust, heat oven to 425°F. Prick bottom and side thoroughly with fork (50 times) to prevent shrinkage.

By 1912, Crisco® was being widely advertised as "An absolutely new product—a scientific discovery which will affect every kitchen in America."

2. Bake at 425°F for 10 to 15 minutes or until lightly browned.

For Unbaked Pie Crusts
1. For recipes using unbaked pie crust, follow baking directions given in each recipe.

For Double Crust Pies
1. Divide dough in half. Roll each half separately. Transfer bottom crust to pie plate. Trim edge even with pie plate.

2. Add desired filling to unbaked pie crust. Moisten pastry edge with water. Lift top crust onto filled pie. Trim ½ inch beyond edge of pie plate. Fold top edge under bottom crust. Flute. Cut slits in top crust to allow steam to escape. Bake according to specific recipe directions.

Bavarian Rice Cloud with Bittersweet Chocolate Sauce

1 envelope unflavored gelatin
1½ cups skim milk
3 tablespoons sugar
2 cups cooked rice
2 cups frozen light whipped topping, thawed
1 tablespoon almond-flavored liqueur
½ teaspoon vanilla extract
Vegetable cooking spray
Bittersweet Chocolate Sauce (recipe follows)
2 tablespoons sliced almonds, toasted

Sprinkle gelatin over milk in small saucepan; let stand 1 minute or until gelatin is softened. Cook over low heat, stirring constantly, until gelatin dissolves. Add sugar and stir until dissolved. Add rice; stir until well blended. Cover and chill until the consistency of unbeaten egg whites. Fold in whipped topping, liqueur, and vanilla. Spoon into 4-cup mold coated with cooking spray. Cover and chill until firm. Unmold onto serving platter. Spoon Bittersweet Chocolate Sauce over rice dessert. Sprinkle with almonds.

Makes 10 servings

Bittersweet Chocolate Sauce

3 tablespoons cocoa
3 tablespoons sugar
½ cup low-fat buttermilk
1 tablespoon almond-flavored liqueur

Combine cocoa and sugar in small saucepan. Add buttermilk, mixing well. Place over medium heat; cook until sugar dissolves. Stir in liqueur; remove from heat.

Favorite recipe from **USA Rice Council**

Original Banana Pudding

½ cup sugar
3 tablespoons all-purpose flour
Dash salt
4 eggs
2 cups milk
½ teaspoon vanilla extract
43 NILLA® Wafers
5 to 6 ripe bananas, sliced (about 4 cups)

Reserve 2 tablespoons sugar. In top of double boiler, combine remaining sugar, flour and salt. Beat in 1 whole egg and 3 egg yolks; reserve 3 egg whites. Stir in milk. Cook, uncovered, over boiling water, stirring constantly 10 minutes or until thickened. Remove from heat; stir in vanilla.

In bottom of 1½-quart round casserole, spoon ½ cup custard; cover with 8 wafers. Top with generous layer of sliced bananas; pour ⅔ cup custard over bananas. Arrange 10 wafers around outside edge of dish; cover custard with 11 wafers. Top with sliced bananas and ⅔ cup custard. Cover custard with 14 wafers; top with sliced bananas and remaining custard.

In small bowl, with electric mixer at high speed, beat reserved egg whites until soft peaks form. Gradually add reserved 2 tablespoons sugar, beating until mixture forms stiff peaks. Spoon on top of custard, spreading to cover entire surface.

Bake at 425°F for 5 minutes, or until surface is lightly browned. Garnish with additional banana slices if desired. Serve warm or cold.

Makes 8 servings

Bavarian Rice Cloud with Bittersweet Chocolate Sauce

Fudgy Rocky Road Ice Cream

5 (1-ounce) squares unsweetened chocolate, melted
1 (14-ounce) can EAGLE® Brand Sweetened Condensed Milk (NOT evaporated milk)
2 teaspoons vanilla extract
2 cups (1 pint) BORDEN® or MEADOW GOLD® Half-and-Half
2 cups (1 pint) BORDEN® or MEADOW GOLD® Whipping Cream, unwhipped
1½ cups CAMPFIRE® Miniature Marshmallows
¾ cup chopped peanuts

In large mixer bowl, beat chocolate, sweetened condensed milk and vanilla until well blended. Stir in remaining ingredients. Pour into ice cream freezer container. Freeze according to manufacturer's instructions. Freeze leftovers.   *Makes about 2 quarts*

Let the Good Times Roll Pinwheels

1 quart softened ice cream, any flavor
1½ cups TEDDY GRAHAMS® Graham Snacks, any flavor, divided
1 quart softened sherbet, any flavor
Chocolate fudge sauce, for garnish
Prepared whipped topping, for garnish
Colored sprinkles, for garnish

Spread ice cream evenly on 15½×10½×1-inch baking pan lined with waxed paper; sprinkle with 1¼ cups graham snacks. Freeze until firm, about 40 minutes. Spread sherbet over graham snack layer. Freeze until firm, about 2 to 3 hours.

Beginning at short end, roll up frozen layers, removing waxed paper; place on serving dish. Cover and freeze at least 1 hour.

To serve, garnish with chocolate fudge sauce, whipped topping, sprinkles and remaining graham snacks. Slice and serve immediately.
Makes 12 servings

Easy Fresh Lemon Ice Cream

2 cups heavy cream or whipping cream or half-and-half
1 cup sugar
Grated peel of 1 SUNKIST® Lemon
⅓ cup fresh squeezed lemon juice

In large bowl, combine cream and sugar; stir to dissolve sugar. Add lemon peel and juice; continue stirring. (Mixture will thicken slightly.) Pour into shallow pan; freeze until firm, about 4 hours. Serve in dessert dishes. Garnish with fresh mint leaves and strawberries, if desired.   *Makes 6 to 10 servings*

Lemon and Fruit Variation: Stir ½ cup mashed strawberries, bananas or kiwifruit into slightly thickened lemon mixture before freezing. Makes about 3½ cups.

It was in 1937 in the kitchen of a Massachusett's country inn that the first chocolate chip cookie emerged. This scrumptious concoction was an immediate hit at the inn and wherever else the recipe spread, but the cookies remained a homemade treat. In 1963, Nabisco introduced Chips Ahoy!® Chocolate Chip Cookies, the company's first commercially produced chocolate chip cookie with homemade flavor. The product name came about when a simple play on words captured everyone's imagination. The nautical cry "Ships ahoy!" became a descriptive boast of chip-laden cookies, "Chips Ahoy!"

Chipwiches

24 CHIPS AHOY!® Chocolate Chip Cookies
3 cups any flavor ice cream, sherbet, frozen yogurt or whipped topping
Sprinkles, chocolate chips, chopped nuts, toasted or tinted coconut, or other assorted small candies

Spread ice cream about ¾ inch thick on flat side of one cookie. Place another cookie on top. Roll or lightly press edges in sprinkles. Repeat. Freeze until firm, about 4 hours.
Makes 12 servings

Peanut Butter Chipwiches: Spread about 1 tablespoon peanut butter on flat side of each of two Chips Ahoy!® Cookies. Place banana slice in center of peanut butter on one cookie; top with other cookie, peanut butter side down. Continue as above.

Cherry Cheesecake Ice Cream

1 (3-ounce) package cream cheese, softened
1 (14-ounce) can EAGLE® Brand Sweetened Condensed Milk (NOT evaporated milk)
2 cups (1 pint) BORDEN® or MEADOW GOLD® Half-and-Half
2 cups (1 pint) BORDEN® or MEADOW GOLD® Whipping Cream, unwhipped
1 (10-ounce) jar maraschino cherries, well drained and chopped (about 1 cup)
1 tablespoon vanilla extract
½ teaspoon almond extract

In large mixer bowl, beat cheese until fluffy. Gradually beat in sweetened condensed milk until smooth. Add remaining ingredients; mix well. Pour into ice cream freezer container. Freeze according to manufacturer's instructions. Freeze leftovers.
Makes about 1½ quarts

Great-Tasting Cookies & Candies

Everyone loves cookies! Who can resist family favorites like luscious chocolate chip, old-fashioned sugar, fudgy brownie and yummy peanut butter cookies? Discover how these cookies, candies and bars can add a special touch to any get-together.

Chewy Brownie Cookies

1½ cups firmly packed light brown sugar
⅔ CRISCO® Stick (⅔ cup)
1 tablespoon water
1 teaspoon vanilla
2 eggs
1½ cups all-purpose flour
⅓ cup unsweetened baking cocoa
¼ teaspoon baking soda
½ teaspoon salt
2 cups semi-sweet chocolate chips
   (12-ounce package)

1. **Heat** oven to 375°F. **Place** sheets of foil on countertop for cooling cookies.

2. **Combine** brown sugar, shortening, water and vanilla in large bowl. **Beat** at medium speed of electric mixer until well blended. **Beat** eggs into creamed mixture.

3. **Combine** flour, cocoa, baking soda and salt. Mix into creamed mixture at low speed just until blended. **Stir** in chocolate chips.

4. **Drop** rounded measuring tablespoonfuls of dough 2 inches apart onto ungreased baking sheet.

5. **Bake** one baking sheet at a time at 375°F for 7 to 9 minutes, or until cookies are set. DO NOT OVERBAKE. **Cool** 2 minutes on baking sheet. **Remove** cookies to foil to cool completely.

Makes about 3 dozen cookies

Chewy Brownie Cookies

Original Nestlé® Toll House® Chocolate Chip Cookies

2¼ cups all-purpose flour
1 teaspoon baking soda
1 teaspoon salt
1 cup (2 sticks) butter, softened
¾ cup granulated sugar
¾ cup packed brown sugar
1 teaspoon vanilla extract
2 eggs
2 cups (12-ounce package) NESTLÉ® TOLL HOUSE® Semi-Sweet Chocolate Morsels
1 cup chopped nuts

COMBINE flour, baking soda and salt in small bowl. Beat butter, granulated sugar, brown sugar and vanilla in large mixer bowl. Add eggs, one at a time, beating well after each addition; gradually beat in flour mixture. Stir in morsels and nuts. Drop by rounded tablespoons onto ungreased baking sheets.

BAKE in preheated 375°F oven 9 to 11 minutes or until golden brown. Let stand for 2 minutes; remove to wire racks to cool completely.

Makes about 5 dozen cookies

Pan Cookie Variation: Prepare dough as above. Spread into greased 15×10-inch jelly-roll pan. Bake in preheated 375°F oven 20 to 25 minutes or until golden brown. Cool in pan on wire rack. Makes about 4 dozen bars.

Slice and Bake Cookie Variation: Prepare dough as above. Divide in half; wrap in waxed paper. Chill 1 hour or until firm. Shape each half into 15-inch log; wrap in waxed paper. Chill for 30 minutes.* Cut into ½-inch-thick slices; place on ungreased baking sheets. Bake in preheated 375°F oven 8 to 10 minutes or until golden brown. Let stand 2 minutes; remove to wire racks to cool completely. Makes about 5 dozen cookies.

*May be stored in refrigerator for up to 1 week or in freezer for up to 8 weeks.

NestléFoods® *The Nestlé® Toll House®*

Morsels story began in the 1930s when Ruth Wakefield, owner of the Toll House Inn, broke bits of a Nestlé Semi-Sweet chocolate bar into her cookie dough. She expected the chocolate "morsels" to melt, but instead they held their shape, softening slightly to a delicate, creamy texture. Thus the Toll House Cookie was born. The rest is history! Ruth Wakefield's recipe has appeared on more than 2 billion packages of Nestlé Toll House Morsels.

Original Nestlé® Toll House® Chocolate Chip Cookies

Peanut Blossoms

1 bag (9 ounces) HERSHEY᾽S KISSES®
Milk Chocolates
½ cup shortening
¾ cup REESE'S® Creamy or Crunchy
Peanut Butter
⅓ cup granulated sugar
⅓ cup packed light brown sugar
1 egg
2 tablespoons milk
1 teaspoon vanilla extract
1½ cups all-purpose flour
1 teaspoon baking soda
½ teaspoon salt
Granulated sugar

Heat oven to 375°F. Remove wrappers from chocolate pieces. In large mixer bowl, beat shortening and peanut butter until well blended. Add ⅓ cup granulated sugar and brown sugar; beat until light and fluffy. Add egg, milk and vanilla; beat well.

Stir together flour, baking soda and salt; gradually add to peanut butter mixture. Shape dough into 1-inch balls. Roll in granulated sugar; place on ungreased cookie sheet. Bake 10 to 12 minutes or until lightly browned. Immediately place chocolate piece on top of each cookie, pressing down so cookie cracks around edges. Remove from cookie sheet to wire rack. Cool completely.

Makes about 4 dozen cookies

Hershey's 100th anniversary logo.

Irresistible Peanut Butter Cookies

1¼ cups firmly packed light brown sugar
¾ cup creamy peanut butter
½ CRISCO® Stick (½ cup)
3 tablespoons milk
1 tablespoon vanilla
1 egg
1¾ cups all-purpose flour
¾ teaspoon salt
¾ teaspoon baking soda

1. **Heat** oven to 375°F. **Place** sheets of foil on countertop for cooling cookies.

Irresistible Peanut Butter Cookies

2. **Combine** brown sugar, peanut butter, shortening, milk and vanilla in large bowl. **Beat** at medium speed of electric mixer until well blended. **Add** egg. **Beat** just until blended.

3. **Combine** flour, salt and baking soda. **Add** to creamed mixture at low speed. Mix just until blended.

4. **Drop** by heaping teaspoonfuls of dough 2 inches apart onto ungreased baking sheet. **Flatten** slightly in crisscross pattern with tines of fork.

5. **Bake** one baking sheet at a time at 375°F for 7 to 8 minutes, or until set and just beginning to brown. DO NOT OVERBAKE. **Cool** 2 minutes on baking sheet. **Remove** cookies to foil to cool completely.

Makes about 3 dozen cookies

Chewy Oatmeal Cookies

¾ **BUTTER FLAVOR* CRISCO® Stick**
  (¾ cup)
1¼ cups firmly packed light brown sugar
 1 egg
⅓ cup milk
1½ teaspoons vanilla
 3 cups quick cooking oats, uncooked
 1 cup all-purpose flour
½ teaspoon baking soda
½ teaspoon salt
¼ teaspoon ground cinnamon
 1 cup raisins
 1 cup coarsely chopped walnuts

*Butter Flavor Crisco® is artificially flavored.

1. **Heat** oven to 375°F. **Grease** baking sheets with shortening. **Place** sheets of foil on countertop for cooling cookies.

2. **Combine** shortening, brown sugar, egg, milk and vanilla in large bowl. **Beat** at medium speed of electric mixer until well blended.

3. **Combine** oats, flour, baking soda, salt and cinnamon. **Mix** into creamed mixture at low speed just until blended. **Stir** in raisins and nuts.

4. **Drop** rounded tablespoonfuls of dough 2 inches apart onto baking sheet.

5. **Bake** one baking sheet at a time at 375°F for 10 to 12 minutes, or until lightly browned. DO NOT OVERBAKE. **Cool** 2 minutes on baking sheet. **Remove** cookies to foil to cool completely.

Makes about 2½ dozen cookies

Cherry Cashew Cookies

 1 cup butter or margarine, softened
¾ cup granulated sugar
¾ cup packed brown sugar
 1 teaspoon vanilla extract
 2 eggs
2¼ cups all-purpose flour
 1 teaspoon baking soda
 1 package (10 ounces) vanilla milk chips (about 1⅔ cups)
 1 cup broken, salted cashews
1½ cups dried tart cherries

Preheat oven to 375°F.

In large mixer bowl, combine butter, granulated sugar, brown sugar, vanilla and eggs. Mix with electric mixer on medium speed until thoroughly combined. Combine flour and baking soda; gradually add flour mixture to butter mixture. Stir in vanilla milk chips, cashews and dried cherries. Drop by rounded tablespoonfuls onto ungreased baking sheets.

Bake 12 to 15 minutes or until light golden brown. Cool on wire racks and store in airtight container.

Makes 4½ dozen cookies

*Favorite recipe from **Cherry Marketing Institute, Inc.***

Chewy Oatmeal Cookies

Reese's® Chewy Chocolate Cookies

2 cups all-purpose flour
¾ cup HERSHEY₃S Cocoa
1 teaspoon baking soda
½ teaspoon salt
1¼ cups (2½ sticks) butter or margarine, softened
2 cups sugar
2 eggs
2 teaspoons vanilla extract
1⅔ cups (10-ounce package) REESE'S® Peanut Butter Chips

Heat oven to 350°F. Stir together flour, cocoa, baking soda and salt. In large mixer bowl, beat butter and sugar until light and fluffy. Add eggs and vanilla; beat well. Gradually add flour mixture, beating well. Stir in peanut butter chips. Drop by rounded teaspoonfuls onto ungreased cookie sheet. Bake 8 to 9 minutes. *(Do not overbake; cookies will be soft. They will puff while baking and flatten while cooling.)* Cool slightly; remove from cookie sheet to wire rack. Cool completely.
Makes about 4½ dozen cookies

Pan Recipe: Spread batter in greased 15½×10½×1-inch jelly-roll pan. Bake at 350°F, 20 minutes or until set. Cool completely in pan on wire rack; cut into bars. Makes about 4 dozen bars.

Ice Cream Sandwiches: Prepare Chewy Chocolate Cookies as directed; cool. Press small scoop of vanilla ice cream between flat sides of cookies. Wrap and freeze.

Located near Chicago, Sokol & Company manufactures and markets Solo and Baker brand retail products as well as ingredients for the baking industry. Solo & Baker fruit and nut cake and pastry fillings can be found in the baking section of the supermarket. The company was established in 1895 by John A. Sokol and has been continuously operated by his family for four generations. Sokol & Company celebrated their centennial year in 1995.

Chocolate-Dipped Almond Horns

1 can SOLO® Almond Paste
3 egg whites
½ cup superfine sugar
½ teaspoon almond extract
¼ cup plus 2 tablespoons all-purpose flour
½ cup sliced almonds
5 squares (1 ounce each) semisweet chocolate, melted and cooled

Preheat oven to 350°F. Grease 2 cookie sheets; set aside. Break almond paste into small pieces and place in medium bowl or food processor container. Add egg whites, sugar and almond extract. Beat with electric mixer or process until mixture is very smooth. Add flour and beat or process until blended.

Spoon almond mixture into pastry bag fitted with ½-inch (#8) plain tip. Pipe mixture into 5- or 6-inch crescent shapes on prepared cookie sheets, about 1½ inches apart. Sprinkle with sliced almonds.

Bake 13 to 15 minutes or until edges are golden brown. Cool on cookie sheets on wire racks 2 minutes. Remove from cookie sheets and cool completely on wire racks. Dip ends of cookies in melted chocolate and place on aluminum foil. Let stand until chocolate is set.

Makes about 16 cookies

Snow-Covered Almond Crescents

1 cup (2 sticks) margarine or butter, softened
¾ cup powdered sugar
½ teaspoon almond extract *or*
    2 teaspoons vanilla
1¾ cups all-purpose flour
¼ teaspoon salt (optional)
1 cup QUAKER® Oats (quick or old fashioned, uncooked)
½ cup finely chopped almonds
    Powdered sugar

Preheat oven to 325°F. Beat margarine, sugar and almond extract until fluffy. Add flour and salt; mix until well blended. Stir in oats and almonds. Using level measuring tablespoonfuls, shape dough into crescents. Bake on ungreased cookie sheet 14 to 17

minutes or until bottoms are light golden brown. Remove to wire rack. Sift additional powdered sugar generously over warm cookies. Cool completely. Store tightly covered.

Makes about 3 dozen cookies

Quaker Oats

The Quaker man was America's first registered trademark for a breakfast cereal. The name was chosen when Quaker Mill partner Henry Seymour found an encyclopedia article on Quakers and decided that the qualities described—integrity, honesty and purity—provided an appropriate identity for his company's oat product. In the late 1800s, Seymour joined forces with two other Midwest milling companies to form The Quaker Oats Company. They began to process and sell high-quality oats that were superior in quality to the oats sold in open barrels at general stores.

Ultimate Sugar Cookies

1¼ cups granulated sugar
1 BUTTER FLAVOR* CRISCO® Stick
    (1 cup)
2 eggs
¼ cup light corn syrup or regular
    pancake syrup
1 tablespoon vanilla
3 cups all-purpose flour plus
    4 tablespoons, divided
¾ teaspoon baking powder
½ teaspoon baking soda
½ teaspoon salt
    Decorations of your choice:
        granulated sugar, colored sugar
        crystals, frosting, decors, candies,
        chips, nuts, raisins, decorating gel

*Butter Flavor Crisco® is artificially flavored.

1. **Combine** sugar and shortening in large bowl. **Beat** at medium speed of electric mixer until well blended. **Add** eggs, syrup and vanilla. **Beat** until well blended and fluffy.

2. **Combine** 3 cups flour, baking powder, baking soda and salt. **Add** gradually to creamed mixture at low speed. **Mix** until well blended. **Divide** dough into 4 quarters.

3. **Heat** oven to 375°F. **Place** sheets of foil on countertop for cooling cookies.

4. **Spread** 1 tablespoon flour on large sheet of waxed paper. **Place** one-fourth of dough on floured paper. **Flatten** slightly with hands. **Turn** dough over and **cover** with another large sheet of waxed paper. **Roll** dough to ¼-inch thickness. **Remove** top sheet of waxed paper.

5. **Cut** out cookies with floured cutter. **Transfer** to ungreased baking sheet with large pancake turner. **Place** 2 inches apart. **Roll** out remaining dough. **Sprinkle** with granulated sugar, colored sugar crystals, decors or leave plain to frost or decorate when cooled.

6. **Bake** one baking sheet at a time at 375°F for 5 to 9 minutes, depending on the size of your cookies (bake smaller, thinner cookies closer to 5 minutes; larger cookies closer to 9 minutes). DO NOT OVERBAKE. **Cool** 2 minutes on baking sheet. **Remove** cookies to foil to cool completely, then **frost** if desired.
Makes about 3 to 4 dozen cookies

Tip: For well-defined cookie edges, or if dough is too sticky or too soft to roll, do the following. **Wrap** each quarter of dough with plastic wrap. **Refrigerate** 1 hour. **Keep** dough balls refrigerated until ready to roll.

Ultimate Sugar Cookies

The Original Rice Krispies Treats® Recipe

3 tablespoons margarine
1 package (10 ounces, about 40)
    regular marshmallows *or* 4 cups
    miniature marshmallows
6 cups KELLOGG'S® RICE KRISPIES®
    cereal
Vegetable cooking spray

1. Melt margarine in large saucepan over low heat. Add marshmallows and stir until completely melted. Remove from heat.

2. Add Kellogg's® Rice Krispies® cereal. Stir until well coated.

3. Using buttered spatula or waxed paper, press mixture evenly into 13×9×2-inch pan coated with cooking spray. Cut into squares when cool.

Makes 24 (2-inch-square) treats

Tony's Tiger Bites®

1 package (10 ounces, about 40)
    regular marshmallows *or* 4 cups
    miniature marshmallows
¼ cup margarine
⅓ cup peanut butter
7½ cups (10-ounce package)
    KELLOGG'S® FROSTED FLAKES®
    cereal
Vegetable cooking spray

Microwave Directions:

1. In 4-quart microwave-safe bowl, melt marshmallows and margarine at HIGH 3 minutes, stirring after 1½ minutes.

2. Stir in peanut butter until mixture is smooth. Add Kellogg's® Frosted Flakes® cereal, stirring until well coated.

3. Using buttered spatula or waxed paper, press mixture into 13×9×2-inch pan coated with cooking spray. Cut into 1½×2-inch bars when cool. *Makes 32 bars*

Rich Lemon Bars

1½ cups plus 3 tablespoons unsifted
    flour
½ cup confectioners' sugar
¾ cup cold margarine or butter
1½ cups granulated sugar
4 eggs, slightly beaten
½ cup REALEMON® Lemon Juice from
    Concentrate
1 teaspoon baking powder
Additional confectioners' sugar

Preheat oven to 350°. In medium bowl, combine *1½ cups* flour and *½ cup* confectioners' sugar; cut in margarine until crumbly. Press firmly on bottom of lightly greased 13×9-inch baking pan. Bake 15 minutes or until lightly browned. Meanwhile, in large bowl, combine granulated sugar, eggs, ReaLemon® brand, baking powder and remaining *3 tablespoons* flour; mix well. Pour over hot baked crust; bake 20 to 25 minutes or until lightly browned. Cool. Cut into bars. Sprinkle with additional confectioners' sugar. Store covered in refrigerator.

Makes 24 to 36 bars

Lemon Pecan Bars: Omit 3 tablespoons flour in lemon mixture. Sprinkle ¾ cup finely chopped pecans over top of lemon mixture. Bake and store as above.

Crimson Ribbon Bars

6 tablespoons butter or margarine, softened
½ cup firmly packed brown sugar
1 teaspoon vanilla
½ cup all-purpose flour
¼ teaspoon baking soda
1½ cups rolled oats
1 cup chopped walnuts
½ cup chopped BLUE RIBBON® Calimyrna or Mission Figs
⅓ cup SMUCKER'S® Red Raspberry Preserves

Heat oven to 375°F. Combine butter, brown sugar and vanilla; beat until well blended. Add flour and baking soda; mix well. Stir in oats and walnuts. Reserve ¾ cup mixture for topping. Press remaining oat mixture in 8-inch square baking pan. Combine figs and preserves; spread mixture to within ½ inch of edges. Sprinkle with reserved oat mixture; press lightly.

Bake for 25 to 30 minutes or until golden brown. Cool in pan; cut into bars.

Makes 20 bars

Oreo® Shazam Bars

28 OREO® Chocolate Sandwich Cookies
¼ cup margarine, melted
1 cup shredded coconut
1 cup white chocolate chips
½ cup chopped nuts
1 (14-ounce) can sweetened condensed milk

Finely roll 20 cookies. Mix cookie crumbs and margarine; spread over bottom of 9×9×2-inch baking pan, pressing lightly. Chop remaining cookies. Layer coconut, chips, nuts and chopped cookies in prepared pan; drizzle evenly with condensed milk. Bake at 350°F for 25 to 30 minutes or until golden and set. Cool completely. Cut into bars.

Makes 24 bars

In 1897, Jerome M. Smucker opened a small custom apple cider mill in Orrville, Ohio. As word of his cider spread, he expanded his operation and began making apple butter using a family recipe passed on from his Pennsylvania Dutch grandfather. The apple butter sold well, and in the 1920s, a full line of preserves and jellies was added. Today, the J.M. Smucker Company is the number one producer of jellies, jams, preserves and ice cream toppings in the United States. The company is managed by the third and fourth generations of the Smucker family and the headquarters is still located on the site of the original cider mill.

Chocolate Caramel Bars

Crust

    MAZOLA® No Stick Corn Oil Cooking Spray
- **2 cups flour**
- **¾ cup (1½ sticks) MAZOLA® Margarine or butter, slightly softened**
- **½ cup packed brown sugar**
- **¼ teaspoon salt**
- **1 cup (6 ounces) semisweet or milk chocolate chips**

Caramel
- **¾ cup (1½ sticks) MAZOLA® Margarine or butter**
- **1 cup packed brown sugar**
- **⅓ cup KARO® Light or Dark Corn Syrup**
- **1 teaspoon vanilla**
- **½ cup chopped walnuts**

For Crust: Preheat oven to 350°F. Spray 13×9×2-inch baking pan with cooking spray. In large bowl with mixer at medium speed, beat flour, margarine, brown sugar and salt until mixture resembles coarse crumbs; press firmly into prepared pan. Bake 15 minutes or until golden brown. Sprinkle chocolate chips over hot crust; let stand 5 minutes or until shiny and soft. Spread chocolate evenly; set aside.

For Caramel: In heavy 2-quart saucepan, combine margarine, brown sugar, corn syrup and vanilla. Stirring frequently, bring to a boil over medium heat. Without stirring, boil 4 minutes. Pour over chocolate; spread evenly. Sprinkle with walnuts. Cool completely. Refrigerate 1 hour to set chocolate; let stand at room temperature until softened. Cut into 2×1-inch bars. Store in tightly covered container at room temperature.

Makes about 4 dozen bars

Planters® Nut Bark

- **6 ounces semisweet chocolate or white chocolate**
- **1 cup PLANTERS® Almonds, PLANTERS® Salted Peanuts or PLANTERS® Cashew Halves**

In top of double boiler, over hot *(not boiling),* water, melt chocolate.

Spread Planters® nuts in lightly greased 9-inch square baking pan. Pour melted chocolate over nuts, spreading lightly with spatula. Cool. Break into pieces. Store in airtight container. *Makes ½ pound*

White Chocolate Pecan Corn

- **1 pop & serve bag (3.5 ounces) JOLLY TIME® 100% All Natural Microwave Pop Corn, Butter Flavored or Natural Flavor, popped**
- **8 ounces vanilla flavored candy coating (white chocolate) *or* 1 package (10 ounces) large vanilla flavored baking chips**
- **½ cup pecan halves**

Place popped pop corn in large bowl. Put candy coating in 1-quart glass measuring cup. Microwave on HIGH 1 to 1½ minutes, or until candy coating is shiny; stir to melt completely. Stir in pecans. Add mixture to pop corn and mix well. Spread on cookie sheet; allow to cool completely.

Makes about 2 quarts

Baked Caramel Corn

Baked Caramel Corn

Nonstick cooking spray
6 quarts popped JOLLY TIME® Pop Corn
1 cup butter or margarine
2 cups firmly packed brown sugar
½ cup light or dark corn syrup
1 teaspoon salt
½ teaspoon baking soda
1 teaspoon vanilla

Preheat oven to 250°F. Coat bottom and sides of large roasting pan with nonstick cooking spray. Place popped pop corn in roasting pan. In heavy saucepan, slowly melt butter; stir in brown sugar, corn syrup and salt. Bring to a boil, stirring constantly; boil without stirring 5 minutes. Remove from heat; stir in baking soda and vanilla. Gradually pour over popped pop corn, mixing well. Bake 1 hour, stirring every 15 minutes. Remove from oven; cool completely. Break apart and store in tightly covered container.

Makes about 6 quarts

Teddy Grahams®, a line of bear-shaped snack cookies, captured the popularity of teddy bears in a bite-size form. This fun-to-eat, wholesome snack for kids comes in three whimsical teddy bear shapes and three flavors—honey, cinnamon and chocolate. Teddy Grahams were the first major line of miniature cookies. Although small in size, they are big in taste!

Barking Bears

7 ounces white confectionary coating
1 cup Chocolate TEDDY GRAHAMS®
    Graham Snacks, divided
7 ounces milk chocolate or light cocoa
    confectionary coating
1 cup Cinnamon TEDDY GRAHAMS®
    Graham Snacks, divided

In small saucepan, over very low heat, melt white confectionary coating. Remove from heat and stir in ½ cup chocolate graham snacks; set aside.

In another small saucepan, over very low heat, melt milk chocolate confectionary coating. Remove from heat; stir in ½ cup cinnamon graham snacks. On lightly

greased, waxed paper-lined 13×9×2-inch baking pan, alternately spoon both mixtures. With fork, gently swirl together to marble and spread mixture into thin layer. Sprinkle with remaining graham snacks. Let stand until firm. Break into pieces. Store in airtight container.   *Makes about 1 pound*

Chex® Muddy Buddies® Brand Snack

9 cups of your favorite CHEX® brand
    cereals (Corn, Rice, Wheat, Double,
    Multi-Bran and/or Graham)
1 cup semi-sweet chocolate chips
½ cup peanut butter
¼ cup margarine or butter
1 teaspoon vanilla extract
1½ cups powdered sugar

1. Pour cereals into large bowl; set aside.

2. In small saucepan over low heat, melt chocolate chips, peanut butter and margarine until smooth, stirring often. Remove from heat; stir in vanilla.

3. Pour chocolate mixture over cereal, stirring until all pieces are evenly coated. Pour cereal mixture into large resealable plastic food storage bag with powdered sugar. Seal securely and shake until all pieces are well coated. Spread on waxed paper to cool.

Makes 9 cups

Note: Do not use reduced-fat margarine or butter; it may cause chocolate mixture to clump and will not coat cereal mixture evenly.

The Ultimate Caramel Apple

1 cup water
1 cup sugar
½ cup heavy cream
6 Red Delicious or Golden Delicious apples
3 ounces white chocolate, finely chopped
3 ounces semi-sweet chocolate, finely chopped
¼ cup coarsely chopped natural pistachios
Red hot cinnamon candies or other small candy
Edible gold dragées

1. In medium, heavy saucepan, combine water and sugar. Over low heat, stir mixture gently until sugar is completely dissolved. Increase heat to medium-low; cook, without stirring, until mixture is dark amber. Remove from heat; slowly stir in heavy cream (mixture will bubble up and spatter a bit). Set aside until barely warm and thickened.

2. Insert popsicle sticks or small wooden dowels into bottom center of apples. Use 10-inch-square piece styrofoam as a stand for apples; cover top of styrofoam with waxed paper to catch caramel drippings.

3. Dip top half of each apple into thickened caramel; stand caramel-topped apples on styrofoam, allowing caramel to run down sides; refrigerate to harden. Meanwhile, melt white chocolate in top of double boiler of gently simmering water; stir until smooth. Transfer melted chocolate to pastry bag fitted with small writing tip. Drizzle thin, random lines of melted chocolate over each apple. Repeat melting and drizzling with semi-sweet chocolate. Decorate each apple with pistachios, candies and gold dragées, if desired. Serve or refrigerate to serve later.

Makes 6 caramel apples

Favorite recipe from **Washington Apple Commission**

The Washington Apple Commission

People around the world who have only a vague idea where Washington state is, know that it's the place where they grow those apples. The image of Washington as one of the top apple-growing regions of the world, and of Washington apples as an international standard of excellence is due to the Washington Apple Commission. Founded in 1937 and headquartered in Wenatchee, Washington, the Commission promotes Washington apples through marketing, public relations and health and food communications.

Acknowledgments

The publisher would like to thank the companies and organizations listed below for the use of their recipes and photographs in this publication.

American Dairy Association

American Egg Board

American Lamb Council

American Spice Trade Association

Best Foods, a Division of CPC International Inc.

Blue Diamond Growers

Borden Kitchens, Borden, Inc.

California Table Grape Commission

Canned Fruit Promotion Service, Inc.

Cherry Marketing Institute, Inc.

Chilean Fresh Fruit Association

Colorado Potato Administrative Committee

Cookin' Good

Corte & Co.

The Creamette Company

Cucina Classica Italiana, Inc.

Dean Foods Vegetable Company

Delmarva Poultry Industry, Inc.

Del Monte Foods

Dole Food Company, Inc.

Filippo Berio Olive Oil

Florida Department of Agriculture and Consumer Services, Bureau of Seafood and Aquaculture

Florida Tomato Committee

Golden Grain/Mission Pasta

Healthy Choice®

Heinz U.S.A.

Hershey Foods Corporation

Hunt Food Co.

The HVR Company

Idaho Potato Commission

Jolly Time® Pop Corn

Kellogg Company

The Kingsford Products Company

Kraft Foods, Inc.

Lawry's® Foods, Inc.

Thomas J. Lipton Co.

Minnesota Cultivated Wild Rice Council

MOTT'S® Inc., a division of Cadbury Beverages Inc.

Nabisco, Inc.

National Broiler Council

National Honey Board

National Live Stock & Meat Board

National Pasta Association

National Sunflower Association

Nestlé Food Company

Newman's Own, Inc.

Norseland, Inc.

Northwest Cherry Growers

Pacific Coast Canned Pear Service

The Procter & Gamble Company

The Quaker Oats Company

Ralston Foods, Inc.

RED STAR® Yeast & Products, A Division of Universal Foods Corporation

Sargento Foods Inc.®

The J.M. Smucker Company

Sokol & Company

StarKist Seafood Company

Sunkist Growers

USA Rice Council

Walnut Marketing Board

Washington Apple Commission

Wisconsin Milk Marketing Board

Index

Chicken
Almond-Chicken Casserole, 32
Baked Chicken with Red-Peppered
 Onions, 50
Buffalo Chicken Wings, 4
Chicken Breasts Diavolo, 52
Chicken Kabobs, 6
Chicken Marsala, 53
Chicken Morocco, 44
Chicken Noodle Soup, 22
Chicken Po' Boy Sandwich, 110
Chicken Saté, 6
Classic Arroz con Pollo, 30
Classic Fried Chicken, 49
Coq au Vin, 28
Country Herb Roasted Chicken, 50
Creole Chicken Thighs, 48
Curried Chicken and Chilean Fruit
 Salad, 88
Deluxe Fajita Nachos, 6
Double-Coated Chicken, 46
Easy Chicken Pot Pie, 30
Golden Gate Chinese Chicken and
 Cabbage Sesame Salad, 88
Hunter-Style Chicken, 50
Lemon Herbed Chicken, 48
Magically Moist Chicken, 48
Oven Tender Chicken™, 46
Simple Marinated Chicken Breasts,
 53
Skillet Chicken Vesuvio, 54
Soft Shell Chicken Tacos, 112
Stuffed Chicken with Apple Glaze,
 46
Tarragon Chicken with Asparagus,
 52
White Bean Stew, 26
Chicken Breasts Diavolo, 52
Chicken Kabobs, 6
Chicken Marsala, 53
Chicken Morocco, 44
Chicken Noodle Soup, 22
Chicken Po' Boy Sandwich, 110
Chicken Saté, 6
Chilean Raspberry and Blueberry Pie,
 155
Chili
Arizona Pork Chili, 24
Chili con Carne Winchester, 24
Sock-It-To-'Em Chili, 24
Chili con Carne Winchester, 24
Chipwiches, 167
Chive Vinaigrette, 101
Chocolate
Barking Bears, 184
Bittersweet Chocolate Sauce, 164

Cappuccino Cake, 140
Carnation® Famous Fudge, 136
Chewy Brownie Cookies, 168
Chex® Muddy Buddies® Brand
 Snack, 184
Chocolate Caramel Bars, 182
Chocolate Cream Torte, 130
Chocolate Crumb Crust, 149
Chocolate-Dipped Almond Horns,
 176
Chocolate Lover's Cheesecake, 148
Chocolate Mayonnaise Cake, 128
Cocoa Cheesecake, 148
Double-Decker Fudge, 134
Foolproof Dark Chocolate Fudge,
 137
Fudgy Rocky Road Ice Cream, 166
German Sweet Chocolate Cake, 126
Hot Fudge Pudding Cake, 127
Marble Cheesecake, 149
Milk Chocolate Fudge, 136
Mint Chocolate Fudge, 136
Mott's® Marble Brownies, 132
Nutty Rich Cocoa Fudge, 134
Old-Fashioned Chocolate Cake, 128
One Bowl® Brownies, 132
Original Nestlé® Toll House®
 Chocolate Chip Cookies, 170
Peanut Blossoms, 172
Planters® Nut Bark, 182
Reese's® Chewy Chocolate Cookies,
 176
Rich Cocoa Fudge, 134
Ultimate Caramel Apple, The, 185
Wellesley Fudge Cake, 124
Chocolate Caramel Bars, 182
Chocolate Cream Torte, 130
Chocolate Crumb Crust, 149
Chocolate-Dipped Almond Horns, 176
Chocolate Lover's Cheesecake, 148
Chocolate Mayonnaise Cake, 128
Chorizos with Onions à la Gonzalez,
 42
Citrus Vinaigrette, 100
Classica™ Fontina Potato Surprise, 82
Classic Arroz con Pollo, 30
Classic Coconut-Pecan Filling and
 Frosting, 128
Classic Crisco® Crust, 162
Classic Fried Chicken, 49
Classic Macaroni and Cheese, 32
Classic Sour Cream Cheesecake, 150
Cocoa Cheesecake, 148
Coconut Lime Pie, 162
Colorful Veg-All® Cornbread, 117
Company's Coming Fish Roll-Ups, 60

Cookies
Cherry Cashew Cookies, 174
Chewy Brownie Cookies, 168
Chewy Oatmeal Cookies, 174
Chocolate-Dipped Almond Horns,
 176
Irresistible Peanut Butter Cookies,
 172
Original Nestlé® Toll House®
 Chocolate Chip Cookies, 170
Peanut Blossoms, 172
Reese's® Chewy Chocolate Cookies,
 176
Snow-Covered Almond Crescents,
 177
Ultimate Sugar Cookies, 178
Cookies 'n' Cream Cheesecake,
 146
Cool 'n Easy Pie, 160
Coq au Vin, 28
Country Fare Breakfast with
 Wisconsin Fontina, 104
Country Herb Roasted Chicken, 50
Country-Style Pot Roast, 36
Crab & Shrimp Quiche, 107
Creamed Spinach à la Lawry's®, 80
Creamy Dijon Vinaigrette, 101
Creamy Key Lime Tart, 158
Creamy Mexican Dressing con
 Cilantro, 100
Creamy Strawberry Cheesecake,
 151
Creole Chicken Thighs, 48
Crimson Ribbon Bars, 181
Crowd-Sized Spinach Soufflé, 106
Crumb Topping, 155
Crusts
Chocolate Crumb Crust, 149
Classic Crisco® Crust, 162
Flaky Pastry Crust, 156
Graham Crust, 148
Cucumber Dill Dip, 12
Curried Chicken and Chilean Fruit
 Salad, 88
Curried Turkey with Pear Chutney,
 56

Deluxe Fajita Nachos, 6
Dips & Spreads
California Seafood Dip, 12
Cucumber Dill Dip, 12
Famous Lipton® California Dip,
 The, 12
French Onion Dip, 12
Guacamole, 11
Hot Artichoke Spread, 15

Metric Chart

VOLUME MEASUREMENTS (dry)

$^1/_8$ teaspoon = 0.5 mL
$^1/_4$ teaspoon = 1 mL
$^1/_2$ teaspoon = 2 mL
$^3/_4$ teaspoon = 4 mL
1 teaspoon = 5 mL
1 tablespoon = 15 mL
2 tablespoons = 30 mL
$^1/_4$ cup = 60 mL
$^1/_3$ cup = 75 mL
$^1/_2$ cup = 125 mL
$^2/_3$ cup = 150 mL
$^3/_4$ cup = 175 mL
1 cup = 250 mL
2 cups = 1 pint = 500 mL
3 cups = 750 mL
4 cups = 1 quart = 1 L

VOLUME MEASUREMENTS (fluid)

1 fluid ounce (2 tablespoons) = 30 mL
4 fluid ounces ($^1/_2$ cup) = 125 mL
8 fluid ounces (1 cup) = 250 mL
12 fluid ounces (1$^1/_2$ cups) = 375 mL
16 fluid ounces (2 cups) = 500 mL

WEIGHTS (mass)

$^1/_2$ ounce = 15 g
1 ounce = 30 g
3 ounces = 90 g
4 ounces = 120 g
8 ounces = 225 g
10 ounces = 285 g
12 ounces = 360 g
16 ounces = 1 pound = 450 g

DIMENSIONS

$^1/_{16}$ inch = 2 mm
$^1/_8$ inch = 3 mm
$^1/_4$ inch = 6 mm
$^1/_2$ inch = 1.5 cm
$^3/_4$ inch = 2 cm
1 inch = 2.5 cm

OVEN TEMPERATURES

250°F = 120°C
275°F = 140°C
300°F = 150°C
325°F = 160°C
350°F = 180°C
375°F = 190°C
400°F = 200°C
425°F = 220°C
450°F = 230°C

BAKING PAN SIZES

Utensil	Size in Inches/Quarts	Metric Volume	Size in Centimeters
Baking or Cake Pan (square or rectangular)	8 × 8 × 2	2 L	20 × 20 × 5
	9 × 9 × 2	2.5 L	22 × 22 × 5
	12 × 8 × 2	3 L	30 × 20 × 5
	13 × 9 × 2	3.5 L	33 × 23 × 5
Loaf Pan	8 × 4 × 3	1.5 L	20 × 10 × 7
	9 × 5 × 3	2 L	23 × 13 × 7
Round Layer Cake Pan	8 × 1½	1.2 L	20 × 4
	9 × 1½	1.5 L	23 × 4
Pie Plate	8 × 1¼	750 mL	20 × 3
	9 × 1¼	1 L	23 × 3
Baking Dish or Casserole	1 quart	1 L	—
	1½ quart	1.5 L	—
	2 quart	2 L	—